W9-AFP-951

Worms Eat Our Garbage
Classroom Activities for
a Better Environment

Mary Appelhof
Mary Frances Fenton
Barbara Loss Harris

Illustrations

Mary Frances Fenton
Nancy Kostecke

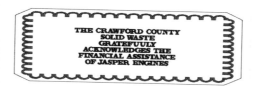

Crawford County
Solid Waste
District
Funded in part
by IDEM

THE CRAWFORD COUNTY
SOLID WASTE
GRATEFUULY
ACKNOWLEDGES THE
FINANCIAL ASSISTANCE
OF JASPER ENGINES

Flower
Press

We thank Dr. Daniel Dindal of the State University of New York, Syracuse, New York, for permission to reprint "Food Web of the Compost Pile," which first appeared in **Ecology of Compost** published by the State University of New York College of Environmental Science and Forestry in 1972.

Several illustrations by Mary Frances Fenton originally appeared in **Worms Eat My Garbage**, (© Flower Press, 1982). These are found on the cover of this book, and on pages 35, 45, 83, 90, 91, 124, 189. We thank her for permission to re-use them here.

Appelhof, Mary, Mary Frances Fenton, and Barbara Loss Harris.
Worms Eat Our Garbage: Classroom Activities for a Better Environment
by Mary Appelhof, Mary Frances Fenton, and Barbara Loss Harris, with illustrations by Mary Frances Fenton and Nancy Kostecke.
First edition.
Kalamazoo, Michigan, USA: Flower Press, © 1993.
232p; ill.; 28 cm
Bibliography: p. 195-196. Appendices, resource materials, teacher's guidelines, glossary, index. ISBN 0-942256-05-0

1. Earthworms 2. Ecology--Juvenile literature 3. Biology
4. Compost 5. Soil science 6. Recycling (waste, etc.)

Worms Eat Our Garbage: Classroom Activities for a Better Environment .
© 1993 by Mary Appelhof.

All rights reserved.
Printed in the United States of America.

Limited reproduction permission: The authors and publisher grant permission to the teachers who purchase this book, or the teacher for whom this book is purchased, to reproduce any part of this book for his or her students.

Other than the situation described above, no part of this book, including illustrations, may be reprinted, photocopied, memory-stored, or transmitted by any means without written permission from the publisher. Brief quotations embodied in critical articles or reviews are permissible.

First edition.

Published by Flower Press
10332 Shaver Road
Kalamazoo, Michigan 49002
U.S.A.

ISBN 0-942256-05-0   10 9 8 7 6 5 4

Printed on 50% recycled paper.

Acknowledgments

Worms Eat Our Garbage is the synergistic product of students, educators, and scientists who shared their expertise with us.

Our special thanks go to the scientists who reviewed our book and provided detailed feedback and specific technical advice:

Dan Dindal, Ph.D., Distinguished Teaching Professor, College of Environmental Science and Forestry, State University of New York, Syracuse, New York

Michael Bisesi, Ph.D., Associate Professor, School of Allied Health and School of Medicine, Medical College of Ohio, Toledo, Ohio

Beverley Diane Van Praagh B.Sc (Hons), Invertebrate Survey Department, Museum of Victoria, Victoria, Australia

We are grateful to these educators for their careful review of the book, their inspirational support, and suggestions for improvement:

Kim Davison, Lincoln School for International Studies, Kalamazoo, Michigan

Steve Fryling, Vicksburg Water Partners Program, Vicksburg Community School, Vicksburg, Michigan

Barbara Hannaford, Gagie School, Kalamazoo, Michigan

Our appreciation goes to these educators who shared with us their field-tested teaching ideas and student products:

Kim Davison, Lincoln School for International Studies, Kalamazoo, Michigan (Elementary Mathematics awardee for work with worms in the classroom: Presidential Award for Excellence in Teaching, 1991).

Gerri Faivre, East Woods School, Oyster Bay, New York (author of an article on vermicomposting in the classroom; January,1993 issue of *Science and Children*)

Sam Hambly, Camp Allsaw, Downsview, Ontario, Canada

Lois Kamoi, Estabrook/New Horizon School, Ypsilanti, Michigan

Our thanks to **Maria Perez-Stable**, Associate Professor, Western Michigan University, Kalamazoo, Michigan and **Cheryl des Montaignes** for their thorough proofing of the text.

Many thanks go to students **Melissa Howe** for allowing us to publish her excellent research which won first place for outstanding achievement in the Kalamazoo Non-Public Schools Science Fair program, 1992, and to **Peter Avram** for his delightful cartoons.

Mary Frances Fenton designed the cover and was primarily responsible for illustrations, charts, typesetting, and general organization of page production. **Mary Appelhof** and **Barbara Harris** also contributed greatly in all areas of book production. We thank each other. Our thanks to **Nancy Kostecke** for her clever art work.

Worms Eat Our Garbage uses a new process called RepKover for its binding. While creating a more durable product, it allows pages to lie open and flat for use as a personal workbook or for photocopying. Each page is perforated. Our thanks to the printer, Malloy Lithographing, Inc.

And finally we thank the students whose photographs appear on the back cover: Estabrook/New Horizon School: Peter Avram, Ryan Bogarin, Leslie Frame, Amanda Jackson, Ryan Landt, Lewis Scott, Shantae Williams; East Woods School: John Garver, Jr., Roddy Lindsay, Jonathon Russ, Abby Weir; Holt High School: Gary Sherman, Darnell Powers, Blew Cribbis, Cali Lodge, Serena Johnson, and Jill Greenman.

Preface

When were you first introduced to an earthworm? In our youth most of us made our first casual acquaintance with one in the garden or at the end of a fishing pole. Perhaps our first serious academic exposure was in an early science class. In fact it may have been the only living animal with which we dealt in our biology courses. In these classes, as with most biota, we learned so little from these early encounters. Now you have within your grasp a most appealing, comprehensive, and exciting discourse that raises the knowledge of earthworms, their biology and their role as an educational instrument to an all time high!

Even though this book was prepared as a teaching aid for elementary and middle school grades, its potential use extends far beyond. Anyone who is fascinated and wishes to learn more about earthworms, as well as those whose active quest is to be an exciting and creative educator, will be served well by this book.

A wealth of biological information is presented within a cleverly presented Wormformation box preceding each activity. In most cases this foundation material coupled with completing the activity leads logically and scientifically to a development of valuable concepts and principles. Besides an obvious emphasis on directions for scientific experiments, the philosophy and practice of use of the scientific method is woven throughout the various exercises. Therefore, problem solving is constantly encouraged. Self-discovery is stimulated. Many experiments are open-ended to further pursuit by the academically gifted. As a teaching guide it is unusually versatile. Each page (which is usually a specific activity) can stand alone or it may be utilized with other activities to suit the teacher's goals. Also the teacher of sensory impaired students should be able to directly use or slightly modify the exercises for their special needs. All experiments are non-invasive to the well-being of the creatures.

The teaching possibilities beyond the scientific realm incorporate a multitude of disciplines including geography, environmental history, planning, mathematics and ratios, visual discrimination, creative writing, vocabulary, poetry and prose, decoding, music and humor. Such interdisciplinary approaches greatly support and emphasize the interrelationships necessary for solving our human and environmental dilemmas.

Also after study and pre-planning by the teacher, it will be found that the concepts and principles originating from many of these studies will provide those ideal laboratory processes that satisfy curricular requirements dictated by state education boards, regents groups or required standardized tests.

Finally, in addition to providing classroom activities for traditional elementary and middle school levels, a number of activities lend themselves for use in high school situations, camping programs, environmental education centers, recycling groups, and master composter programs. They may also provide enjoyment to the amateur naturalist and gardener. Many individuals, school systems and communities should be much wiser and the environmental conditions in our land should be greatly benefitted by the use of this innovative manual on this dynamic master of the soil--our earthly annelid!

Daniel L. Dindal, Ph.D.
Distinguished Teaching Professor
Soil Ecology
State University of New York
College of Environmental Science
  and Forestry
Syracuse, New York

February 1993

Prologue
Why Worms?

As we were nearing completion of this curriculum guide and activity book and reviewing it to determine what concepts we still needed to address, co-author Barbara Harris asked me, "Why worms?"

Garbage-eating worms provide a logical solution to a wide range of problems. Worms have been converting organic residues to again usable form for 300 million years. We bypass this natural recycling process when we flush garbage down the drain, incinerate it, or bury it in landfills where it may not decompose for decades.

We place unnecessary burdens on our water supply when we use eight gallons of water to dilute a pound of food waste in a garbage disposal underneath the sink. Wastewater treatment plants require more chemicals, produce more sludge, and consume more energy to process the increased volume of water brought in from garbage disposals. It takes energy and resources to transport and dispose of the sludge, often so contaminated with heavy metals and other toxics that disposal on agricultural land is not wise.

Burial of organic waste in landfills presents problems as well. It takes up space, nearly 18% of the waste stream is yard waste (leaves and grass clippings), another 7-8% food waste. Landfills are not only expensive to operate, they are becoming extremely difficult to site near residential areas because citizens fear the degradation of their environment with noise, heavy traffic, polluted drinking water, odors, and blowing papers and plastic. Decomposition of organic materials in the absence of oxygen produces methane gas which has potential for explosion when not dealt with adequately.

Incineration of garbage reduces the volume of waste. But it carries unacceptable risks. Toxic flue gases permeate not only the immediate atmosphere, but also the atmosphere continents away from where the burning takes place. The remaining ash which must be buried is often so toxic that burial in a hazardous waste landfill is required. Incinerators are expensive to build and operate, often placing intolerable financial burdens on citizens.

All of the garbage disposal methods described above--wastewater treatment plants, landfills, or incinerators--destroy the resource present in organic waste. The problem is in trying to dispose of it. The solution is to make use of it. Hence, worms.

Worms provide a simple, yet effective, means to convert organic waste into a nutrient-rich material capable of supporting plant growth. They do it efficiently, noiselessly, and without complaint. Because worms can do it where the garbage is produced, in home, office, or school, no hauling and central processing is required. Plants grown on the vermicompost from a worm bin make use of the nutrients present in the organic waste, thus reducing the need for synthetic fertilizers. This on-site technique is simple, effective, and convenient. It saves water, energy, landfills, and soil. It is instructive. But, best of all, it is fun. What better way to contribute in a positive way to our environment than to have **Worms Eat Our Garbage**?

To the learners who become scientists
as a result of using this book.

Introduction

Publication of **Worms Eat My Garbage** in 1982 started a slow, but steadily increasing groundswell of interest in garbage-eating worms. Thousands of people from across the United States and Canada used the 100-page manual to set up and maintain a system for processing organic waste by means of redworms.

As author and publisher of **Worms Eat My Garbage,** I interact with hundreds of worm bin users. Through phone calls, letters, and direct conversations, people share their experiences with me. Three groups of people stand out because of the intensity of their interest: teachers who want to use worm bins in their classroom, parents (or kids) who see the possiblity of a great science fair project with worms, and people who are concerned with using Earth's resources wisely.

Worms Eat Our Garbage: Classroom Activities for a Better Environment responds to many requests for specific classroom activities related to earthworms. I have encouraged teachers and youth leaders to keep me informed of their experiences. Teachers report that a classroom worm composting bin excites children. They love the worms. Disappearance of the garbage after a few weeks amazes the students. Some change what they bring to lunch so they can have leftovers to feed the worms. Children see that the worm bin is truly recycling in action when they can bury lunch scraps one month, harvest compost another month, and grow a plant in the compost two months later.

The excitement children feel as they learn more about worms stimulates creative expression. Worm puppets, worm costumes, worm songs, and plays with worms as main characters have all come from classroom worm projects. The enthusiasm carries through to the community, as well. At least a dozen teachers sent me newspaper and journal articles showing their students with classroom worm bins.

To make this classroom activities book as useful and comprehensive as possible, I collaborated with two fine educators, Mary Frances Fenton, and Dr. Barbara Harris, from the College of Education at Western Michigan University. Mary Frances, Professor Emeritus, spent over 30 years as a media specialist and graphics consultant. She illustrated **Worms Eat My Garbage.** She is now an avid gardener and a certified organic grower. Barb trains teachers in the field of special education and has written children's activity books appropriate for both the gifted and for children with learning disabilities. She teaches graduate and undergraduate courses in assessment and curriculum. I bring to the task several years of biology teaching, 20 years of experience working with worms, an insatiable curiosity, and a commitment to "change the way the world thinks about garbage."

We organized the book into three sections, The World of Worms, Worms at Work, and Beyond the Bin.

> The World of Worms introduces earthworms, how they are named, kinds of worms, their needs, habitat, physical and behavioral characteristics, and how they relate to other things in the natural world.

> Worms at Work presents the concept of worms eating garbage in a controlled environment (vermiculture) by means of a story. A series of

activities takes students through weighing the organic waste from lunch, setting up a worm bin, making observations, and determining what kinds of food are suitable for worms. Although a worm bin will enhance learning, many of the hands-on activities can be done without a worm bin. Because the work of worms in natural environments is to recycle organic nutrients in soil, we provide a series of activities related to soil, including soil profiles, worm growth in soils, and the effect of earthworms on soil fertility, aeration, and plant growth.

Beyond the Bin expands the range of activities for the learner beyond the worm bin experience. This section includes activities on making use of worm castings as plant food, how removal of organic waste from the waste stream can save landfills, and recycling and other solid waste alternatives.

Over 400 illustrations, both computer-generated and hand-drawn, appear throughout this book. Our philosophy is that the illustrations must teach and inform in addition to providing visual interest to the page.

We designed **Worms Eat Our Garbage** as a transdisciplinary curriculum to integrate science concepts with art, reading, mathematics, geography, language, and history. Science subjects related to the earthworm include biology, ecology, zoology, and soil science. A map illustrating the integration of curriculum content appears on the inside front cover of the book; a map showing content relationships appears on the inside back cover.

Activity pages have specific components.

- **Wormformation** provides background information.

- **Materials** identifies the items needed.

- **Directions** provides sequenced steps.

- **Bonus Activity** enriches and extends the activity.

- **Skill area(s)** appear on the lower right corner.

Teacher pages give record sheets, bulletin board ideas, answers, additional content, and tips for certain activities. We provide a list of resources and enrichment materials, a comprehensive glossary, bibliography, and an index.

As much as the publication of a book represents completion of a task, we know that, in many ways, it is only the beginning of another. We honor the learning which took place as we developed this book. And we salute the learning which will come from it. Enjoy, and please share your use of this book with us.

- Mary Appelhof, with Mary Frances Fenton and Barbara Harris

Table of Contents

The World of Worms

Learner Outcomes

After completing the activities in this unit, the student will:

- understand the physical characteristics of the earthworm

- understand the behavior of the earthworm

- understand the needs of the earthworm

- understand the habitat of the earthworm

- understand the relationship of the
  plant, mineral, and animal kingdoms to the earthworm

Wormformation

The shape of a worm is long and thin. It has a soft body and it has no bones beneath its skin. The body of a worm is made of many little rings with grooves between them. Each of these rings is called a segment. Each segment has bristles called setae that help the worm move. A worm has no arms, legs, or eyes.

Posterior (Tail End)   *segments*   *Anterior (Head End)*   *prostomium "flap"* — *mouth* — *setae* — *clitellum*

Directions

Read the *Wormformation* and look at the earthworm diagram to answer the questions. *(Hint: Use the glossary for extra help.)*

1. What is the basic shape of a worm?_____

2. Does a worm have arms or legs?_____

3. Does a worm have a mouth?_____

4. The prostomium is a flap above the worm's_____

5. Does a worm have eyes?_____

6. What is the head end of a worm called?_____

7. What is the tail end of a worm called? _____

8. What is the name of the swollen band?_____

9. What are the rings on a worm's body called?_____

10. The bristles that aid in a worm's movement are called_____

Bonus Activity Look at a real worm. Identify its parts.

> Observing the earthworm should be done with great care. Attending to the worm's needs will let you do experiments with little or no stress to this creature. A worm is stressed by a shining light, by surroundings that are too dry, and by being too hot or too cold.
>
> ### Wormformation

Directions
Read the Wormformation and follow the steps described below.

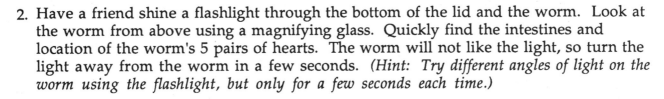

Materials

- 1 clear, plastic lid
- 1 t (teaspoon) water
- 1 magnifying glass
- 1 live earthworm (a young worm is more transparent that a mature one)
- 1 flashlight

Procedure

1. Put a worm on the clear lid. Wet the worm with water to keep its skin moist.

2. Have a friend shine a flashlight through the bottom of the lid and the worm. Look at the worm from above using a magnifying glass. Quickly find the intestines and location of the worm's 5 pairs of hearts. The worm will not like the light, so turn the light away from the worm in a few seconds. (*Hint: Try different angles of light on the worm using the flashlight, but only for a few seconds each time.*)

3. Return the worm to its moist bedding before going to step 4.

4. Draw the worm in the space below. Label the intestines and hearts.

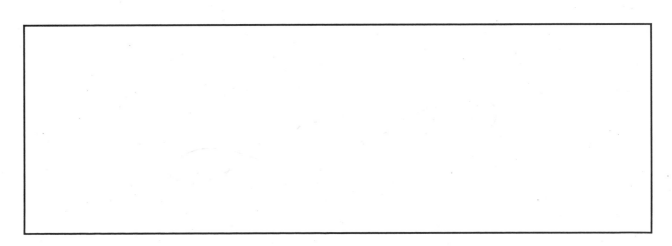

Bonus Activity Observe and label other parts of the worm drawing, such as head end, tail end, and clitellum.

Directions

Feel a worm. Look at a worm. Listen to a worm. Smell a worm. Describe your worm in words in the Worm Word Portrait. Write a word list from your worm portrait on the lines below.

○ Worm Word Portrait

My Word List _____   _____

_____   _____

_____   _____

_____   _____

Bonus Activitiy

Look up your words in a thesaurus. Write the synonyms in your worm word portrait.

Name_____

Wormformation
An earthworm can grow only <u>so</u> long. Its maximum length as a well-fed adult will depend on what kind of worm it is and how many segments it has. Short worms have fewer segments than long worms.

Directions
Use the chart to answer the questions below.

		81 mm (average length)
Eisenia fetida	Range 32-130 mm	Redworm (common name)
		110 mm (average length)
Allolobophora caliginosa	Range 80-140 mm	Southern Worm (common name)
		124 mm (average length)
Octolasion cyaneum	Range 68-180 mm	Woodland Blue Worm (common name)
		195 mm
Lumbricus terrestris	Range 90-300 mm	Nightcrawler or Dew Worm (common name)

Centimeters

Inches

1. What is the scientific name of the longest worm? *Lumbricus terrestris*

2. What is the common name of the shortest worm? *Eisenia fetida*

3. In what habitat can you find the worm which is of medium length? *southern worm 3cm*

4. One of the longest worms in the world is the giant earthworm of Australia. It can be 12 times longer than a redworm. What is its length in centimeters? *300 cm*

5. How long is the southern worm? Give your answer in inches. *80-140?*

6. According to the chart, if you find a worm 7 inches long, what kind of worm is it most likely to be? *Red worm*

Wormformation

All things in the natural world can be classified into three kingdoms.

1. Plants — Plants produce their own food and are green at some stage of their lives. They reproduce. Plants do not move about the way animals can. A dandelion is a plant.

2. Animals — Animals live by eating the bodies of other organisms, whether plant or animal. Animals reproduce. Most animals have body parts that allow them to move. A turtle is an animal.

3. Minerals — Minerals require no food and do not reproduce. Minerals are inert which means they are inactive and unable to move by themselves. Minerals do not eat. Chalk is a mineral.

Directions

Read the Wormformation above. Write plant, animal or mineral after each riddle.

What is my Kingdom?

I swim in the ocean and eat small fish._____

I fly in the air and swim in a pond._____

I am the desert floor._____

Fish swim in me._____

I am a milk jug and can be recycled._____

I am graphite. Your pencil point is made of me._____

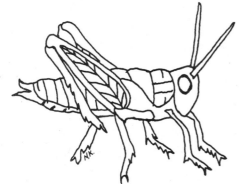

I live in the ground and come out at night to search for food._____

You see your face when you look into my reflective surface._____

I grow in the woods and have bark and leaves. _____

I hang upside down to sleep. _____

Bonus Activity Identify a plant, animal, or mineral for each riddle above.

WORMS EAT OUR GARBAGE Copyright © 1993 Flower Press   Classification

Wormformation

What is a worm? When you think of a worm, what do you think of? Do you think of an earthworm, or do you think of some other kind of worm? Many animals are called worms, but the kind of worm called an earthworm has special characteristics and lives in the soil.

As an animal, the earthworm moves by itself. It moves in search of food or to avoid danger. You may have seen a worm try to get away from a bird. The bird finds an earthworm a tasty meal. The worm cannot run away because it has no legs or feet.

The shape of a worm is long and thin. It has a soft body, and it has no bones beneath its skin. If you look at a worm carefully, you will see the skin shines, or glistens. That is because a worm's skin is moist.

Worms do not have eyes to see like we do, but they can sense the difference between light and dark. Because many people like worms, and eyes seem to give worms character, you may see cartoon pictures of worms with eyes. But remember, a real worm has none.

Directions
    Read the **Wormformation** and other references to answer the questions below.

1. There are three kingdoms - plants, animals and minerals. The earthworm is an animal. Name one characteristic which makes it an animal instead of a plant or mineral.

2. What makes worms different from other animals, such as an insect or a bear?

3. Give two events that could cause an earthworm to move.

4. Why does an earthworm glisten?

5. What is the shape of an earthworm's body?

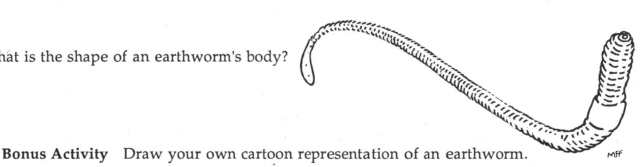

Bonus Activity Draw your own cartoon representation of an earthworm.

Classic Names

Scientists call living things organisms. By using the same system for naming plants and animals, scientists all over the world can talk to each other and share information. Here are some of the rules they follow:

Wormformation

1. The name of each organism consists of two words.
2. The first word is the <u>genus,</u> the second word is the <u>species.</u>
3. Both genus and species names usually come from Latin or Greek.
4. The genus and species names often describe the organism in some way.

Directions

Use the information in the two charts below to answer the questions.

Latin or Greek	English Meanings
fetidus	stinking, ill-smelling
cyano	dark blue
rosa, rosea	pink, a rose
ruber, rubris	red, rubella
terra	earth
turgere	to swell out, turgid
lumbricus	a worm

Scientific Names of Some Worms

- *Lumbricus terrestris*
- *Octolasion cyaneum*
- *Lumbricus rubellus*
- *Eisenia rosea*
- *Eisenia fetida*
- *Apporectodea turgida*

1. Which organism could be called "a worm of the earth?"

   _____

2. Which worm might be called the "woodland blue worm?"

   _____

3. Which two worms might be colored red, reddish-brown, or pink?

   _____

4. Which worm might be described as "filled out and dense, rather than limp?"

   _____

5. People who fish sometimes dislike a foul-smelling substance released from the posterior end of this worm. Based on its name, which worm do you think it might be?

   _____

A dictionary gives this definition for the earthworm:

"Any of various terrestrial annelid worms of the class Oligochaeta and especially of the family Lumbricidae that burrow into and help aerate and enrich soil."

Wormformation

Directions

Many scientific terms are words that come from other languages. We provide English definitions for the Latin or Greek words in the word list which follows. Read the earthworm definition in Wormformation. Then use the word list to find the meaning of the scientific words. Write your "translations" in the blank spaces.

Word List

- aer - air
- annellus - small ring
- chaite - hair
- lumbricus - earthworm
- oligos - few, little
- seta - bristle
- terra - earth

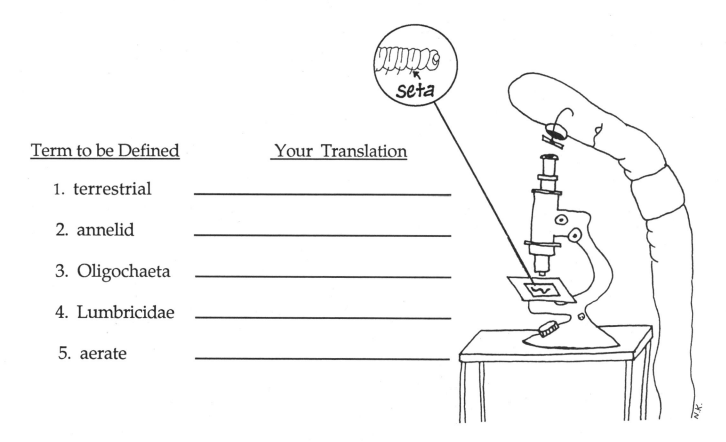

Term to be Defined | Your Translation

1. terrestrial _____

2. annelid _____

3. Oligochaeta _____

4. Lumbricidae _____

5. aerate _____

Bonus Activity Rewrite the definition of the earthworm found in Wormformation. Use your translated terms to make it more understandable.

Wormformation

Scientists call living things organisms. By using the same system for naming plants and animals, scientists all over the world can talk to each other and share information. Here are some of the rules they follow:

1. The name of each organism consists of two words.
2. The first word is the <u>genus</u>, the second word is the <u>species</u>.
3. Both genus and species names usually come from Latin or Greek.
4. The genus-species (scientific name) often describes the organism in some way.

Directions
Use the information in the two charts below to answer the questions.

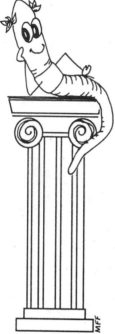

<u>Latin or Greek</u>		<u>English Meanings</u>
chloros	_____	green, yellowish green
longus	_____	long
okto	_____	eight
tetra	_____	four

<u>Scientific Names of Earthworms</u>
Allolobophora chlorotica
Apporectodea longa
Eiseniella tetraedra
Dendrobaena octaedra

---

1. Which worm is called the "octagonal-tail worm?"

   _____

2. Which worm is commonly called the "green worm?"

   _____

3. Which organism is called the "square-tail worm?"

   _____

4. Which worm is characterized by being long?

   _____

Bonus Activity What is the scientific name of human beings? What does this name mean?

Name_____

Wormformation

Calling earthworms by common names can be confusing. What one person calls a "redworm," you may call a "red wiggler." Your neighbor may call it a "manure worm." Other common names for this same animal are fish worm, dung worm, striped worm, and brandling.

To avoid confusion, scientists use a precise two word system for naming organisms. The first word is the genus (plural: genera). The second word is the species. All organisms of the same genus are more closely related than those of different genera.

Directions

Using references, find the scientific names for the genus and species of each of the cats pictured below.

1.

Cheetah
_____
Common name

_____
Genus   Species

2.

Panther
_____
Common name

_____
Genus   Species

3.

House Cat
_____
Common name

_____
Genus   Species

4.

Tiger
_____
Common name

_____
Genus   Species

5.

Bobcat
_____
Common name

_____
Genus   Species

6.

Lion
_____
Common name

_____
Genus   Species

Bonus Activity   Identify the cats pictured above that are most closely related to each other.

Color Word Chart

(Hint: Sometimes only part of these words is used, such as geo for geolo.)

Word Root	English
chloro	greenish
ruber	red
rosea	pink
cyan	blue
geolo	yellow
lavendula	lavender

Some scientific names of worms and plants describe their characteristics. The worm name, *Lumbricus rubellus*, comes from the Latin language. Part of the name, *ruber*, is a root word which means the color red. One common name for this worm is the red marsh worm.

Wormformation

Directions

Using the Color Word Chart, complete the name of each color in the sentences below. *(Hint: Part of the scientific names are underlined.)*

1. Todd saw a_____ colored worm and knew it

   was the *Allolobophora chlorotica*.

2. The bird, *Geothlypis trichas*, is a warbler with a

   _____ throat.

3. Mohammad found a worm with a bluish tint to its body.

   He guessed it was an *Octolasion _____ eum*.

4. Maria's grandmother gave her a_____

   plant for the garden. She labelled it *Lavendula vera*.

5. Joan has an *Acer rubrum* tree growing in her backyard.

   Her father calls it a_____ maple.

6. Shirley named her pet worm "Pinky." She surprised

   her mother when she called it by its scientific name,

   Eisenia _____.

Bonus Activity Make up a funny scientific name for an imaginary worm. Use the color chart and the dictionary. Give your worm a common name and draw its picture.

12

Vocabulary

Name_____ **Once a Worm, Always a Worm**

Earthworms are long, thin, soft-bodied animals. They have no bones beneath their skin. Other animals that we also call worms are really insect larvae which change into moths, butterflies, and beetles when they become adults. Earthworms remain worms as adults.

Wormformation

Read the *Wormformation* and use reference books to complete the following chart. Place a check in the proper column to identify whether the common name refers to an earthworm or an insect larva. If the answer is *Insect Larva*, identify the insect it becomes. *(Hint: Redworm is done for you.)*

Earthworm
(Place a check by each earthworm.)

Insect Larva
(Place a check by each insect larva.)

What insect does it become?

Moth

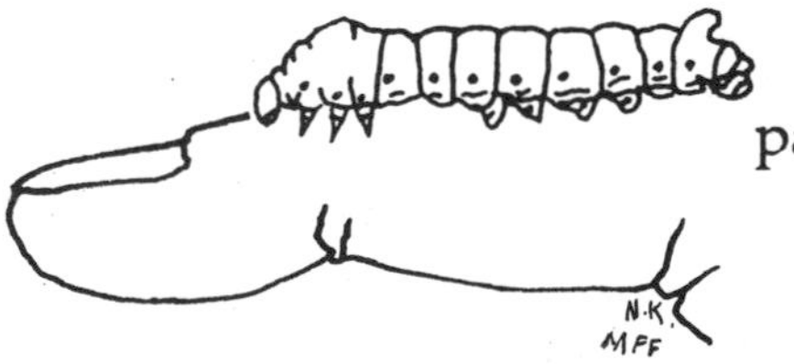

Japanese Beetle Grub

Firefly

Common Names	Earthworm	Insect Larva	What insect does it become?
cabbage worm	◯	⬭	_____
redworm	✓	⬭	_____
tomato hornworm	◯	⬭	_____
nightcrawler	◯	⬭	_____
red wiggler	◯	⬭	_____
cutworm	◯	⬭	_____
silkworm	◯	⬭	_____
angleworm	◯	⬭	_____
pasture worm	◯	⬭	_____
mealworm	◯	⬭	_____
corn rootworm	◯	⬭	_____
manure worm	◯	⬭	_____
celeryworm	◯	⬭	_____
grubworm	◯	⬭	_____
corn earworm	◯	⬭	_____

Bonus Activity How would you classify a "*glow worm*?" Is it an insect larva, an adult insect, or an earthworm?

Name_____

Directions

Look at the *actual size* drawing of the giant worm on page 15.
Read the story, and answer the questions that follow.

The Giant Gippsland Earthworm (*Megascolides australis*) is one of the world's largest earthworms. It lives only in a small area in South East Australia. Adult worms are approximately 1000 mm long. Their diameter is about 20 mm. They can weigh up to 381 g. An interesting fact is that the baby giant earthworm takes from 8 to 12 months to hatch from its cocoon.

The Australian government needs more information about this amazing earthworm. They need this information to help decide whether to put the Giant Gippsland Earthworm on the list of endangered species.

Ms. Beverley Van Praagh is a scientist. The World Wildlife Fund supports her research to go on field trips to locate these giant worms. Once she identifies the kind of habitat where the worms live, she travels there with several strong people who can help with the digging. They select a possible site, then start digging, looking for signs of a worm or its burrow. They may dig a hole so deep and long that the diggers require a ladder to climb out.

Sometimes, in the process of digging, a worm is injured and the digging site becomes, literally, a bloody mess. It bothers Ms. Van Praagh to harm the worms in this way. She would welcome another way to conduct her important work without having to injure the worms.

1. How many inches long is the average adult giant earthworm?_____

2. What is the diameter of the giant earthworm in inches?_____

3. How many ounces can a giant earthworm weigh?_____

> 1 mm = 0.039 in.
> 1 g = 0.035 oz

4. The holes the scientists dig to find the giant earthworm are often deeper than the height of an adult person. True or False? What information in the story supports your answer?

_____

5. Why is Ms. Van Praagh studying these giant worms?

_____

6. Suggest other ways Ms. Van Praagh could conduct her work without injuring the worms._____

Name_____

Mega Worm
Megascolides australis

Start

Mega Worm Squirmed in its burrow when it...

Directions
Use references to find
out about other animals
in Australia. Write a story
about some of them. Begin
with the story "starter."
*(Hint: When you get to
the end of the worm
continue your story on
another sheet of paper.)*

M.F.

Wormformation

If you want to see a nightcrawler, go looking for one on your moist lawn with a red or amber light. On a warm, damp night, the hungry worm is out of its deep burrow looking for a tasty leaf or a grassy blade to eat.

Directions

Describe an earthworm by writing an adjective (descriptive word) in each of the segments of the worm below. Use a thesaurus to expand your worm descriptors. *(Hint: Some adjectives are seeing words, like gray, long, and skinny. Some adjectives describe feelings, such as slimy and cool.)*

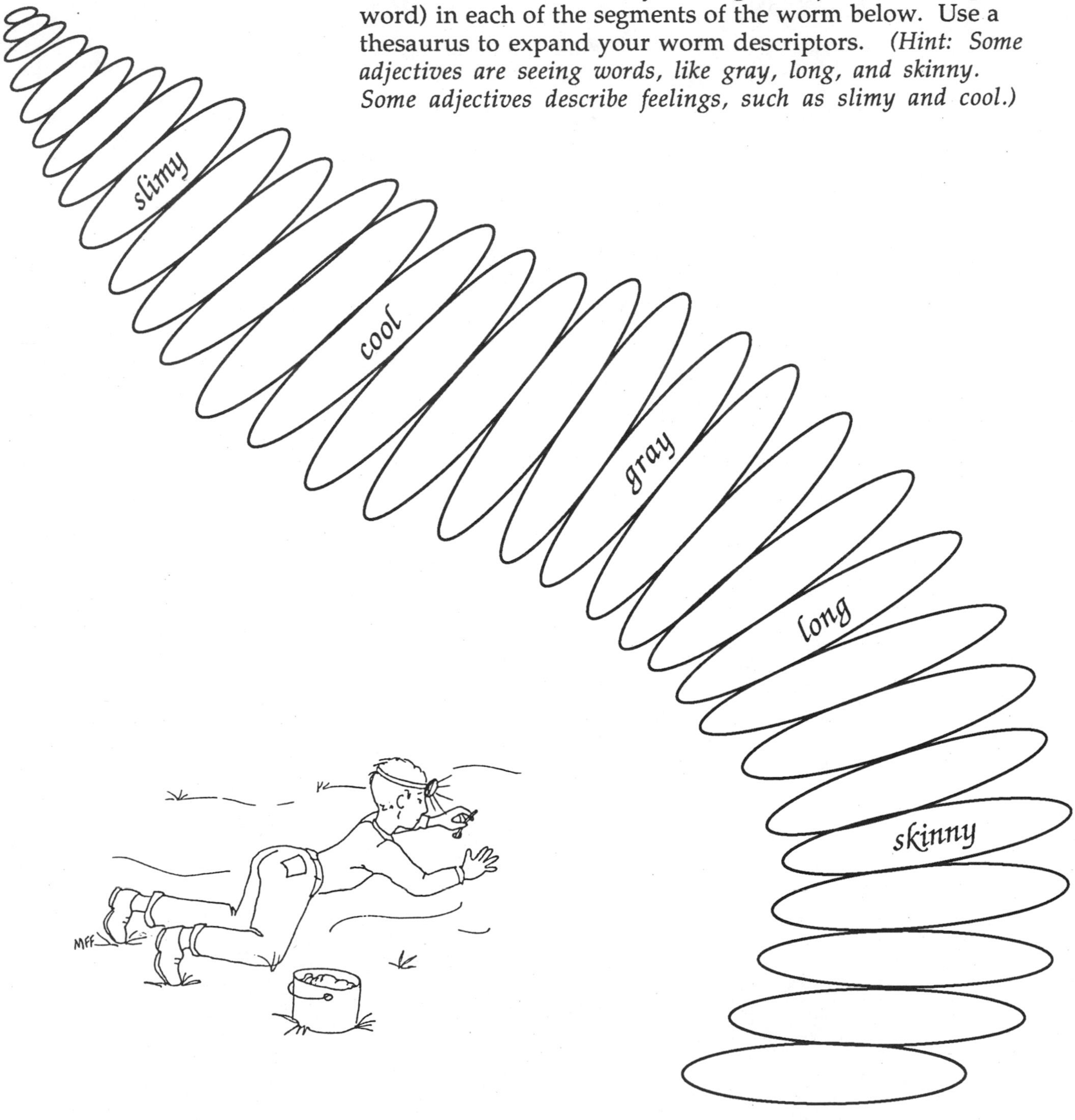

slimy

cool

gray

long

skinny

Bonus Activity Circle all the adjectives in the *Wormformation* above.

Name_____

Wormformation

Baby worms hatch from small lemon-shaped structures called cocoons. Cocoons are yellowish, light brown, or reddish, and about 1/3 the size of a grain of rice.

Cocoon
(Actual size)

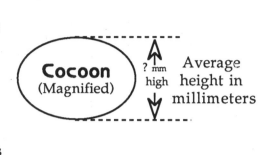

? mm
long

Average
length in
millimeters

Cocoon
(Magnified)

? mm
high

Average
height in
millimeters

B. Directions

Mark an X next to each item you think would be smaller than a cocoon.

☐ lemon

☒ grain of salt

☐ grapefruit

☒ pea

☒ radish seed

☒ beet seed

☒ cabbage seed

☒ carrot seed

☐ avocado pit

☒ apple seed

☒ grape seed

☐ lima bean

A. Directions

Use a metric ruler to measure the length and height of the two cocoons in the **Wormformation.** Answer questions 1 through 7. (Hint: Cut out and use the metric ruler below.)

1. The magnified cocoon is_____ mm high.

2. The magnified cocoon is _____ mm long.

3. It is_____ cm high.

4. It is _____ cm long.

5. The unmagnified cocoon (actual size) is_____ mm high.

6. The unmagnified cocoon (actual size) is _____ mm long.

7. If a cocoon magnified 10 times is 18 mm long, what is its actual size in millimeters?
    _____ mm

Not all cocoons are the same size. Sizes range from 1.75 mm to 6.0 mm long.

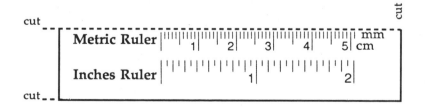

cut

| Metric Ruler | mm |
| Inches Ruler | |

Bonus Activity List at least three things that are about the size of a worm cocoon.

WORMS EAT OUR GARBAGE Copyright © 1993 Flower Press

Math/Measurement

Wormformation

Look at a worm and a cocoon through a strong magnifying lens or a dissecting microscope.   At the very tip of the "head," or anterior end of a worm, is the prostomium. This is the scientific term for the area before the worm's mouth. The word ending "um" means one, or singular. A word ending with the letter "a," as in prostomia, means the word is plural.

A worm's prostomium looks like a flap of skin that hangs over its mouth like a fat lip. Its function is to protect the opening from unwanted objects just as our lips do.

A worm cocoon is the casing from which two to five baby worms will hatch. Cocoons look like tiny, brownish lemons. They are transparent, that is, if a worm is inside you can see it. The opening where the worm will come out appears to have ragged edges.

Directions In *Items 1 & 2* , mark an X on the one drawing that is incorrect in each box.
In *Items 3 to 8* , mark an X on each misspelled or repeated word.

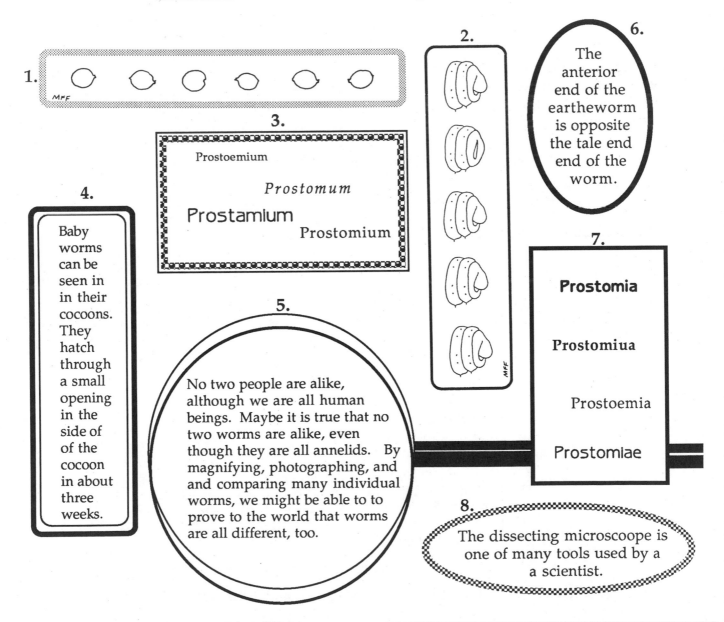

1.

2.

3.
Prostoemium

Prostomum

Prostamium

Prostomium

4.
Baby worms can be seen in in their cocoons. They hatch through a small opening in the side of of the cocoon in about three weeks.

5.
No two people are alike, although we are all human beings. Maybe it is true that no two worms are alike, even though they are all annelids.   By magnifying, photographing, and and comparing many individual worms, we might be able to to prove to the world that worms are all different, too.

6.
The anterior end of the eartheworm is opposite the tale end end of the worm.

7.
Prostomia

Prostomiua

Prostoemia

Prostomiae

8.
The dissecting microscoope is one of many tools used by a a scientist.

Directions
Write a story after each "story starter."

The first time I saw a worm, I _____

_____

_____

_____

_____

_____

The first time I touched a worm, I _____

_____

_____

_____

_____

_____

The first time I saw a worm at work, I _____

_____

_____

_____

_____

_____

Bonus Activity Select the story you like best and share it with a classmate.

Earthworms use setae and two kinds of muscles to move. Like the claws of a cat, setae can be extended or pulled in. The setae act as brakes. These stiff bristles push against a surface and keep that portion of the worm from moving while the muscles contract.

Circular muscles are short and circle the worm's body. When they tighten, the earthworm becomes thinner and longer, squeezing the front end forward.

Other muscles run lengthwise along the body. When these long muscles tighten, they pull the segments closer together. The body shortens and swells. The worm moves forward by first lengthening itself and then drawing the tail section toward the head.

Wormformation

Materials
- wide rubber band (1/4 inch wide) cut to make 1 long strip
- ball point pen

Directions
Lay the strip of rubber flat and use a ball point pen to mark it like this:

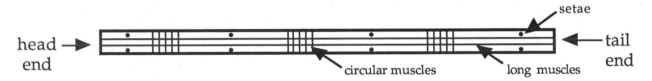

(Note: This model is not exactly like a worm, but it points out important features. Every segment of a real worm has setae and circular muscles.)

1. Draw two lines from one end to the other. These represent the long muscles which reach from one end of the worm to the other.

2. Draw three sets of vertical lines as shown on the diagram. These represent the circular muscles which go around the worm in each segment.

3. Draw eight pairs of short diagonal lines. These represent the setae which are found on each segment of a worm. They serve as worm brakes.

4. Label one end, "head," and the other end, "tail."

5. To make your model worm move, place it on the table and do the following:
   - hold each end of the model between your fingers
   - hold onto the tail end and stretch the head end forward
   - hold the head end against the table and relax the tail end
     (Hint: the tail end will move toward the head end.)
   - Repeat these steps to make your model worm move across the table.

6. Write down your observations of the model worm's movement. Observe an earthworm move. How does the movement of the model worm differ from that of the live worm? How is it the same?

A muscle can either contract or relax. When a muscle contracts, it gets shorter; when it relaxes, it becomes limp. Worms move through contracting and relaxing their muscles in waves, alternating between circular muscles and long muscles.

Contraction of the circular muscles forces the worm's body forward. Think of this. If you fill a balloon with water, tie it, and squeeze it in your hand, you cause it to "balloon out" where you are not squeezing it. The water, under pressure from the muscles in your hand, changes the shape of the balloon. Worms, like the balloon, change their shape by squeezing against body fluids with their circular muscles.

Then, the long muscles contract, drawing the tail end of the worm towards the skinny front end. When the long muscles contract, the circular muscles relax, causing the worm to become thick. To keep from skidding during movement, tiny bristles called setae act as brakes to hold part of the worm's body against the surface. The worm moves forward or backward in similar ways.

As simple as it looks, worm movement is actually very complex.

Wormformation

Directions
    Read the Wormformation. Label the drawings to help explain your written answers to the questions.

1. What does the worm look like in the region where the circular muscles contract or tighten?

Circular Muscles

Circular muscles contract. This increases pressure, and forces front end of worm forward.

2. What happens to the worm when the circular muscles relax?

Long Muscles

3. What happens to the worm when the long muscles contract?

~Long muscles contract   ~Long muscles relax
~Circular muscles relax   ~Circular muscles contract

Setae brakes "on"   Setae brakes "off"

4. What happens to the worm when the long muscles relax?

~Long muscles relax   ~Long muscles contract
~Circular muscles contract   ~Circular muscles relax

5. What purpose do the setae serve?

Setae brakes "on"   Head end pulled back
Setae brakes "off"

Name _____

Directions

Observe a worm move on three different surfaces.
Contrast how fast it moves on the different surfaces, and
the direction it moves. Note the waves of muscle
contractions. What does it do when it meets an obstacle?
Does it move backward? Will it climb up on things?
What seems to be the purpose of a particular movement?
Use a magnifying glass for more detail.

*(Remember to respect the worm's needs. Use several worms one at a
time so that no worm is in the light, in dry air, or on a dry surface very
long.)*

Worms move by hydraulics.
Hydraulics concerns the
movement of fluids under
pressure. Contraction of a
worm's muscles increases
the pressure of its body
fluid, squeezing it forward
into a region where the
muscles are relaxed. This
region looks swollen
compared to the narrow
region with contracting
muscles. **Wormformation**

I want to be a hydraulics engineer when I grow up!

Ideas for types of surfaces that can be wet or dry:

desk top	glass plate	newspaper
plastic pan	clear jar	notebook paper

Observation #1

Type of surface _____ Wet ? _____ Dry? _____ (Check one)

    I observed _____

_____

_____

_____

Observation #2

Type of surface _____ Wet ? _____ Dry? _____ (Check one)

    I observed _____

_____

_____

_____

Observation #3

Type of surface _____ Wet ? _____ Dry? _____ (Check one)

    I observed _____

_____

_____

_____

Wormformation

Unlike humans, earthworms have no lungs. Creatures with lungs <u>breathe</u> by inhaling and exhaling (oxygen and carbon dioxide) gases. Worms cannot breathe, but they do *respire* through the whole surface of their bodies. Oxygen dissolves in the moisture on the worms' bodies. It then passes into the body and the bloodstream. Worms need enough moisture to keep their skins wet, but not enough to drown them. Worms are not aquatic animals, but some species can live under water if there is enough oxygen dissolved in the water. Without moisture, however, the worms will die.

Directions

Read the Wormformation and answer the questions.
Hint: Use **Key Ideas** to help solve the problems.

1. Worms need oxygen and moisture. List three (3) places you might find wild worms.

Key Idea
An aquarium pump adds oxygen to water.

_____

_____

_____

2. Why do worms live in the places you listed above?

Key Idea
Plants in an aquarium produce oxygen in the presence of light.

_____

_____

_____

3. According to the Wormformation, would it be possible for an earthworm to live in water in an aquarium?
   Yes ☐ No ☐

   Under what conditions? _____

Key Idea
Cold water can hold more oxygen than warm water.

_____

_____

4. Will a worm be more likely to survive in warm water or cold water?

   Why? _____

_____

_____

My Day as a Worm

Name _____

Directions
Imagine you are a worm. Complete the sentences below to write your own story.

One night I went to sleep and awoke the next morning as a worm. I didn't know which end was my head. I tried to _____

_____

I slithered out of bed and then _____

_____

_____

Before going to school, I wanted a hearty breakfast. I had a special craving for _____

_____

When I got to school no one recognized me because _____

_____

_____

The teacher saw me wiggling in my seat and said, " _____

_____."

After school, it was raining so I _____

_____

_____

_____

_____

When I awoke the next morning I was a child again. Whenever I see a worm I will _____

_____

_____

_____

_____

A. Answer the questions by circling true or false. Use reference materials for assistance.

True or False   1. Birds and worms are alike because they both have mouths.

True or False   2. Dogs and worms are alike because they both have eyes.

True or False   3. Spiders and worms are alike because they both make cocoons
for their young.

True or False   4. Turtles and worms are alike because they both breathe oxygen.

B. Complete these sentences.

1. a. Horses are like dogs because_____.

   b. Horses are not like dogs because_____.

2. a. Millipedes are like spiders because_____.

   b. Millipedes are not like spiders because_____.

3. a. Cats are like worms because_____.

   b. Cats are not like worms because_____.

4. a. Birds are like worms because_____.

   b. Birds are not like worms because_____.

Warm/Cold Adaptation

Wormformation
Worms are cold-blooded animals, as are snakes, turtles, and fish. Their bodies' temperature depends on the temperature of their surroundings. Worms move more slowly in colder temperatures and may freeze and die at 32°(degrees) F (0° C). Some believe baby worms survive freezing temperatures while in their cocoon stage. As the temperature increases, worms become more active and cocoons hatch. They prefer to crawl, eat, and mate at temperatures in the 60° to 80° F range. Temperatures above 90° F may kill worms.

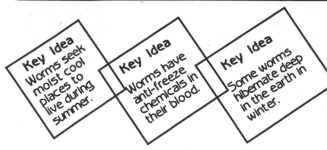

Key Idea Worms seek moist cool places to live during summer.

Key Idea Worms have anti-freeze chemicals in their blood.

Key Idea Some worms hibernate deep in the earth in winter.

Directions
Read the Wormformation and use reference books to answer the questions.

1. Where do worms go during the winter in cold climates?

2. Why do not all wild worms freeze and die in cold climates?

3. How do other cold-blooded animals survive freezing weather?

4. Identify two places worms may go during the summer in hot climates?

5. Why do not all wild worms die in very hot climates?

6. How do other cold-blooded animals survive in very hot weather?

Bonus Activity   Write why you think we warm-blooded humans survive in very hot and very cold climates.

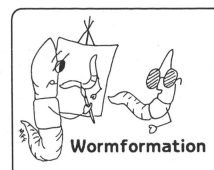

Wormformation

Worms do not have eyes as we do. When you see an artist's cartoon of a worm with eyes you know that the artist is using her imagination. The artist is trying to give the worm expression and personality. Humans show their emotions of happiness, sadness, and surprise with their eyes. Imagine a worm drawing a picture of another worm. A picture drawn by a worm would not show human eyes. Perhaps a worm can sense if another worm is happy or sad by using another part of its body and does not need eyes at all. Scientists who study earthworms know that they sense light without having eyes.

Question
Do worms sense light? Try this experiment.

Materials
You will need the following materials to do your scientific study:

- a shallow container (jar lid)
- black paper or cardboard
- live worm (at least 1)
- moist paper
- towel
- a flashlight

Directions

1. Place moist paper towel in shallow container.

2. Cover half of the container with the cardboard.

3. Put worm in the uncovered portion of the container.

4. Shine the flashlight on the worm.

5. Observe what the worm does.

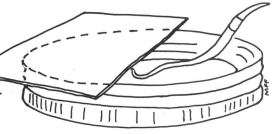

Record your observations in the box below and answer the question.

What did you observe? _____

_____

_____

Does a worm sense light? _____Yes   _____No

How do you know?_____

_____

Bonus Activity   Use a red or amber plastic bag over lighted end of flashlight and observe the reaction of the worm to light. Record what you see the worm doing.

Earthworms eat soil and organic matter. The organic matter nourishes them. The soil passes through their long digestive tract. Organic matter which serves as food for worms includes plant material and the decomposing remains of large and small animals. Worms prefer some foods over others. Because a worm's mouth is very small, it is easy for the worm to eat small organisms like bacteria, protozoa, and fungi. Larger foods must be softened with moisture so the worm can suck the food into its mouth.

Wormformation

Definitions

decompose: to decay, to rot; to break down into smaller particles

digestive tract: the long tube in animals where food is digested (broken down)

nourish: the use of energy from food to promote or sustain growth

organic matter: material which comes from something which was once alive

organism: any individual living thing

soil: loose surface material of the earth in which plants grow

Directions
Use Wormformation and the definitions to answer the questions which follow.

1. Check the items in A. Found in soil which you might find if you looked closely at a _cup_ of soil.

2. Check the items in B. Food for worms which you think would be worm food.

3. Put a second check mark in the box for each worm food you think can be eaten easily.

Menu
Dinners
Bacteria Buns
Protozoa Sandwich
Fungus Soup

	A. Found in a cup of soil	B. Food for worms
sand	◯	▭
an orange	◯	▭
clay	◯	▭
bits of leaves	◯	▭
gravel	◯	▭
plant roots	◯	▭
bacteria	◯	▭
ground rock	◯	▭
tree limb	◯	▭
a rotten seed	◯	▭
dead insect	◯	▭

Bonus Activity Pour a cup of soil on a paper plate and list what you find.

> ## Wormformation
> If worms need air to respire, then there must be air in the earth where worms live. The spaces between particles of soil are not empty spaces; they contain air. Soil and sand are not as solid as they seem.

Purpose

The purpose of this experiment is to find out how much air is contained in the spaces between soil particles.

Materials

- water
- 2 clear measuring cups
- sand
- soil

Directions

1) Measure out 1/2 cup water.

2) Measure out 1/2 cup sand.

3) Pour the water into the cup of sand. *(The combination will measure less than 1 cup, even though two halves equals a whole. This is because there is air between the grains of sand. The water replaces the air.)*

4) To find out the amount of space in the sand occupied by air, subtract the measurement of the mixture of water and sand from 1 cup. The difference is the amount of air that was in the spaces between the grains of sand.

5) Repeat steps 1 through 4 using soil instead of sand.

Observation Record

Write what you saw when you poured the water onto the soil or sand.

Observing Sand -_____

_____

_____

Observing Soil -_____

_____

_____

Conclusions -_____

_____

_____

Observation/Analysis

Name_____   "Breathing" Basics

When we humans breathe, our lungs exchange oxygen molecules in the air for carbon dioxide molecules. We exhale (breathe out) less oxygen and more carbon dioxide. This exchange of gases must take place on moist surfaces which are deep within our lungs. These moist surfaces are called membranes. We also exhale water in the form of very small droplets.

Wormformation

Worms respire through their skin. A worm does not have lungs inside its body as we do. However, exchange of oxygen and carbon dioxide molecules across a worm's skin is similar to that exchange in our lungs. This is why a worm's skin must be moist to allow it to breathe. If a worm's body dries out, it dies because it cannot respire.

Directions
Use the diagram to answer the questions.

Key
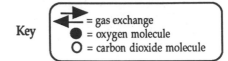
➜ = gas exchange
● = oxygen molecule
○ = carbon dioxide molecule

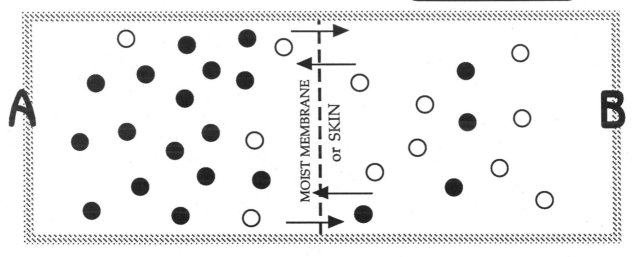

1. How many molecules of oxygen are on the A side of the moist membrane?

2. How many molecules of oxygen are on the B side?_____

3. How many molecules of carbon dioxide are on the B side?____

4. Which side contains the most molecules of oxygen ?_____

5. Molecules can freely move across the membrane from A to B and B to A. When we and the worms "breathe", molecules of one gas try to be equal in number on both sides of membrane or skin. In the diagram above, which way do the molecules move to make both sides equal? Write answers below:

   a. Kind of molecule from A to B?_____ How many?____

   b. Kind of molecule from B to A?_____ How many?____

Moist Membrane

Lungs

Bonus Activity Pick out 5 words from **Wormformation**. Write their definitions using a dictionary.

Directions

Observe a living worm. Use your observations to help you answer the following questions. *Note: Do not stress your worms. Keep their bodies moist and out of the light when you are ready to write your answers.*

Can a worm move backwards?
If yes, describe why a worm will move backwards.

_____

_____

Can a worm move fast?
Describe why it will move fast. _____

_____

What happens when it meets another worm? _____

_____

_____

What does it do when it comes to a rock? _____

_____

_____

Is your worm sensitive to touch?
Describe what makes you
think a worm is sensitive to touch. _____

_____

_____

Can a worm feel? Describe what
makes you think a worm can feel. _____

_____

_____

Can you smell the worm?
Describe what it smells like? _____

_____

_____

Can a worm smell?
Describe why you think
a worm can smell. _____

_____

WORMFORMATION

Earthworms move by themselves. They move in search of mates, to avoid light, or as a result of vibrations. They also move to seek food and to avoid danger.

Directions

Circle the items below that may cause an earthworm to move.

Bonus Activity   List the things in your classroom or home that might cause a worm to move.

WORMS EAT OUR GARBAGE Copyright © 1993 Flower Press

Comprehension

Directions

To find the hidden word, read the statement below and color the spaces as directed. (*Hint: The word is a small, bristle-like structure on a worm's body. It helps the worm move by gripping the surface.*)

5	2	5	8	1	5	2	4	7	8	5	8	3	8	5	7
8	5	7	3	6	8	3	1	6	7	2	6	1	2	4	1
2	4	6	1	7	2	7	3	7	1	8	7	3	5	8	6
8	2	5	2	3	5	8	6	1	3	4	6	1	4	2	3
4	5	8	4	3	2	4						1	1		
1	3	6	5	1	4	7	1	3	6	2	3	2	2	3 7	8 6
6	7	3	8	7	8	6	3	1	7	8	1	5	4	2	1
5	2	5	4	7	2	8	2	6	1	4	6	2	8	5	7
8	2	4	2	6	5	8	4			4	1	4	5 3	6	8

1. If worms have eyes, color the #1 spaces.

2. If worms have mouths, color the #2 spaces.

3. If worms move toward light, color the #3 spaces.

4. If worms have blood, color the #4 spaces.

5. If worms need oxygen from the air, color the #5 spaces.

6. If worms have lungs, color the #6 spaces.

7. If worms live in dry places, color the #7 spaces.

8. If worms' bodies need to be wet, color the #8 spaces.

WORMS EAT OUR GARBAGE Copyright © 1993 Flower Press

Comprehension

Wormformation

Earthworms live in many places on earth. Some climates and conditions, however, do not provide a suitable environment for them.
You rarely find an earthworm in a desert, high on a mountain, or in areas constantly under snow and ice. They don't live in oceans--most species of earthworms cannot tolerate salt water. Earthworm species can spread or migrate from one region to another, but deserts, oceans, mountain ranges, and glaciers serve as barriers to worm migration.

Directions
Answer the following questions based on the *Wormformation* and other references.

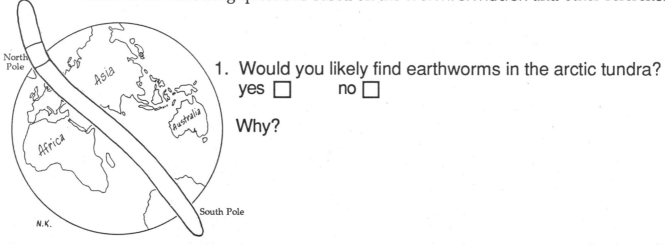

1. Would you likely find earthworms in the arctic tundra?
   yes ☐   no ☐

   Why?

2. What characteristics of a desert make it an unsuitable
   place for an earthworm to live?

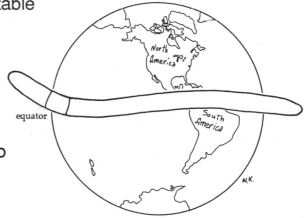

3. If an ocean is a barrier to earthworm migration,
   how do you think European worm species came to
   North America?

4. Would you likely find earthworms in lands along the equator?   yes ☐   no☐

   Why?

Bonus Activity   Use a globe or world map to locate and list earthworm barriers.

WORMS EAT OUR GARBAGE Copyright © 1993 Flower Press   Geography

W O R M F O R M A T I O N

EARTHWORM MATING AND COCOON FORMATION

EACH WORM HAS <u>BOTH</u> OVARIES AND TESTES.

AREA OF OVARIES AND TESTES

CLITELLUM (BAND)

TWO WORMS JOIN BY MUCUS FROM THEIR CLITELLA. SPERM THEN PASS FROM EACH WORM TO THE SPERM STORAGE SACS IN THE OTHER WORM.

OVARIES AND TESTES

CLITELLA

LATER, A COCOON FORMS ON THE CLITELLUM OF EACH WORM. THE WORM BACKS OUT OF THE HARDENING COCOON.

COCOON FORMATION

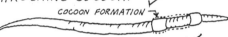

EGGS AND SPERM ARE DEPOSITED IN THE COCOON AS IT PASSES OVER OPENINGS FROM OVARIES AND SPERM STORAGE SACS.

APPROX. 1/8" LENGTH

AFTER BEING RELEASED FROM THE WORM, THE COCOON CLOSES AT BOTH ENDS. EGG FERTILIZATION TAKES PLACE IN THE COCOON.

TWO OR MORE BABY WORMS HATCH FROM ONE END OF THE COCOON.

MFF

Directions
Read the Wormformation, and unscramble the sentences below. Number the sentences in the correct sequence.

Sequence

__1.__   Two worms join together.

_____   A cocoon forms on each worm.

_____   The worm backs out of the cocoon.

_____   The cocoon closes at both ends.

_____   Eggs and sperm are deposited in the cocoon.

_____   The baby worms hatch.

_____   Sperm passes from one worm to the other worm.

Bonus Activity Search for cocoons in your worm bin. Describe them in words or pictures.

Name _____

Directions
To find the hidden word, read the statement below and color the spaces as directed.
(Hint: This is what a worm tries to do when exposed to light.)

1. If circular muscles make the worm get thinner, color the # 1 spaces.

2. If setae serve as brakes, color the # 2 spaces.

3. If a muscle works by contracting, color the #3 spaces.

4. If worms move by means of jointed legs, color the #4 spaces.

5. If long muscles make a worm get fatter, color the #5 spaces.

6. If worms have only one set of circular muscles, color the #6 spaces.

7. If hydraulics is the study of the ecology of worms, color the #7 spaces.

8. If worms have setae on almost all segments, color the #8 spaces.

WORMS EAT OUR GARBAGE Copyright © 1993 Flower Press

Comprehension

> ## Wormformation
> How do you tell the head end of an earthworm from the tail end? The ends seem to be alike because the earthworm has no eyes, no nose, and no ears. It has a mouth which is tiny and hard to see. When the worm moves, the head end usually goes first. The clitellum, the swelling or band that covers several segments, is nearer to its head end than its tail end.

Directions
Complete the chart by: (1) reading the questions in the first column; (2) developing steps to find the answers; and (3) writing the results after you have done the experiment. *(Hint: Experiment #1 has been completed for you.)*

	State the Question	Procedures	Results
	What do you need to know about the worm?	What did you do to find out the answer?	What are the results of your observation and experiment?
Experiment 1	**How did you tell the head end from the tail end?**	I placed a worm on a smooth, wet surface and watched it to see which end moved the most and in what direction.	I watched the worm move for a brief time. The worm moved forward with the head end most of the time. I saw it shrink backwards two times.
Experiment 2	**What does a worm do when it meets an object in its path?**		
Experiment 3	**Does a worm move differently on a dry than on a wet surface?**		

Bonus Activity   Repeat Experiment #1 testing 3 or more worms, one at a time. Record results.

WORMFORMATION

A nightcrawler builds a burrow which extends far down into the ground. This kind of worm feeds on leaves and dead grass. At night, with its tail end secured in its burrow, the nightcrawler weaves its head end back and forth seeking food. Finding something, it grasps the food in its mouth and draws it down into its burrow. The worm knows to grab a leaf by the pointed end so that it will more easily curl through the narrow opening of the burrow. Part of the leaf sticks out of the hole, hiding the mouth of the burrow from view.

Further down, the burrow may have little enlargements, or chambers. These chambers may contain small pebbles and bits of stone, or various seeds. The burrow's walls are smooth, having been lined with worm castings.

Bacteria thrive in a worm's burrow when the ground is moist. Cocoons may be deposited there. Burrow visitors include insects and millipedes.

Directions

Read the Wormformation. Pretend you have shrunk to the size of a worm and have the chance to visit its burrow. Circle the items you are likely to see in the burrow.

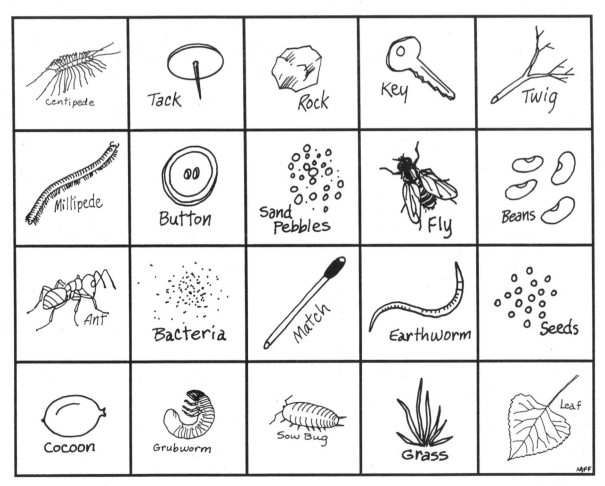

Bonus Activity

Look for signs of worm burrows near the small, irregular clumps of soil which are worm castings. Try to find the burrow opening, or look for leaves which may be pulled into the burrow opening. Describe what you find.

Name_____

> Charles Darwin spent 39 years of his life studying earthworms over 100 years ago. He made careful observations, kept records, and asked questions. He then analyzed his results, drew conclusions, and reported his work to other scientists.
> **Wormformation**

Directions

Read the following paragraphs which Charles Darwin wrote based on his observations of earthworms. Answer the questions below.

Habits of Worms*
by Charles Darwin, 1809-1882

"Earthworms must be considered as terrestrial animals. . . During the summer when the ground is dry, they penetrate to a considerable depth and cease to work, as they do during the winter when the ground is frozen.

Worms are nocturnal in their habits, and at night may be seen crawling about in large numbers, but usually with their tails still inserted in their burrows. By the expansion of this part of their bodies, and with the help of the short . . . bristles, with which their bodies are armed, they hold so fast that they can seldom be dragged out of the ground without being torn into pieces. During the day, they remain in their burrows, except at the pairing season, when those which inhabit adjoining burrows expose the greater part of their bodies for an hour or two in the early morning."

*From Chapter 1: *The Formation of Vegetable Mould through the Action of Worms* by Charles Darwin, 1881.

1. Many kinds of worms are *aquatic* animals; that is, they live in water. Darwin stated that earthworms are *terrestrial* animals. If earthworms are terrestrial animals, where do they live?_____

2. During what two seasons of the year are worms least active?_____

3. What phrase did Darwin use which means that worms are *less active*?_____

4. Worms go deep in their burrows when the ground is _____or _____

5. During a 24-hour period, when are worms most likely to be seen crawling?_____

6. Which end of a worm remains in its burrow while the other end moves around?

_____

7. What parts of a worm's body help the worm hold fast to the inside of its burrow?

_____

8. Where do worms stay during the day?_____

HABITS OF WORMS -- THEIR SENSES

"Worms do not possess any sense of hearing. They took not the least notice of the shrill notes from a metal whistle, which was repeatedly sounded near them; nor did they of the deepest and loudest tones of a bassoon.

They were indifferent to shouts, if care was taken that the breath did not strike them. When placed on a table close to the keys of a piano, which was played as loudly as possible, they remained perfectly quiet."

FROM: *The Formation of Vegetable Mould through the Action of Worms* by Charles Darwin, 1881

Directions

Read the passage written by Charles Darwin. Design and conduct three experiments to answer the question, *Can Worms Hear?* Complete the chart below.

	Question	Procedures	Results
	Can worms hear?	What did you do to find out the answer?	What are the results of your observation and experiment?
Experiment 1			
Experiment 2			
Experiment 3			

Worms are good for the earth for many reasons. Their burrows create channels in the soil. The soil becomes more porous, allowing water to move to greater depth. Such drainage after heavy rains helps to control erosion. Worms help plants to grow better. Plant roots require oxygen, and worm burrows provide passages for air to get next to the roots deep within the ground. We call this function aeration.

Worms which tunnel deeply in the soil bring subsoil closer to the surface, mixing it with topsoil which has more organic matter. Slime, a secretion of earthworms, contains nitrogen, which is an important plant food. The sticky slime helps to hold clusters of soil particles together in formations called aggregates. Soil aggregates (clumps) lying next to each other permit air to move between the spaces.

Wormformation

Directions

Read Wormformation to learn about the reasons worms are good for the Earth. Complete the crossword puzzle. (*Hint: All word answers are in the Wormformation.*)

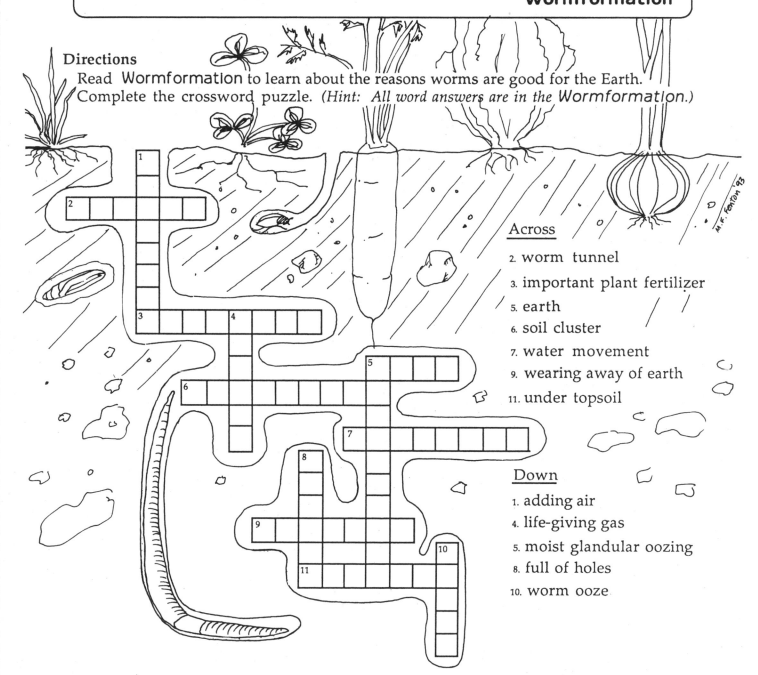

Across

2. worm tunnel
3. important plant fertilizer
5. earth
6. soil cluster
7. water movement
9. wearing away of earth
11. under topsoil

Down

1. adding air
4. life-giving gas
5. moist glandular oozing
8. full of holes
10. worm ooze

Directions
   Some of these pictures
show worms in
unnatural situations.
Circle each error. *(Hint:*
More than one error may
appear in each picture).

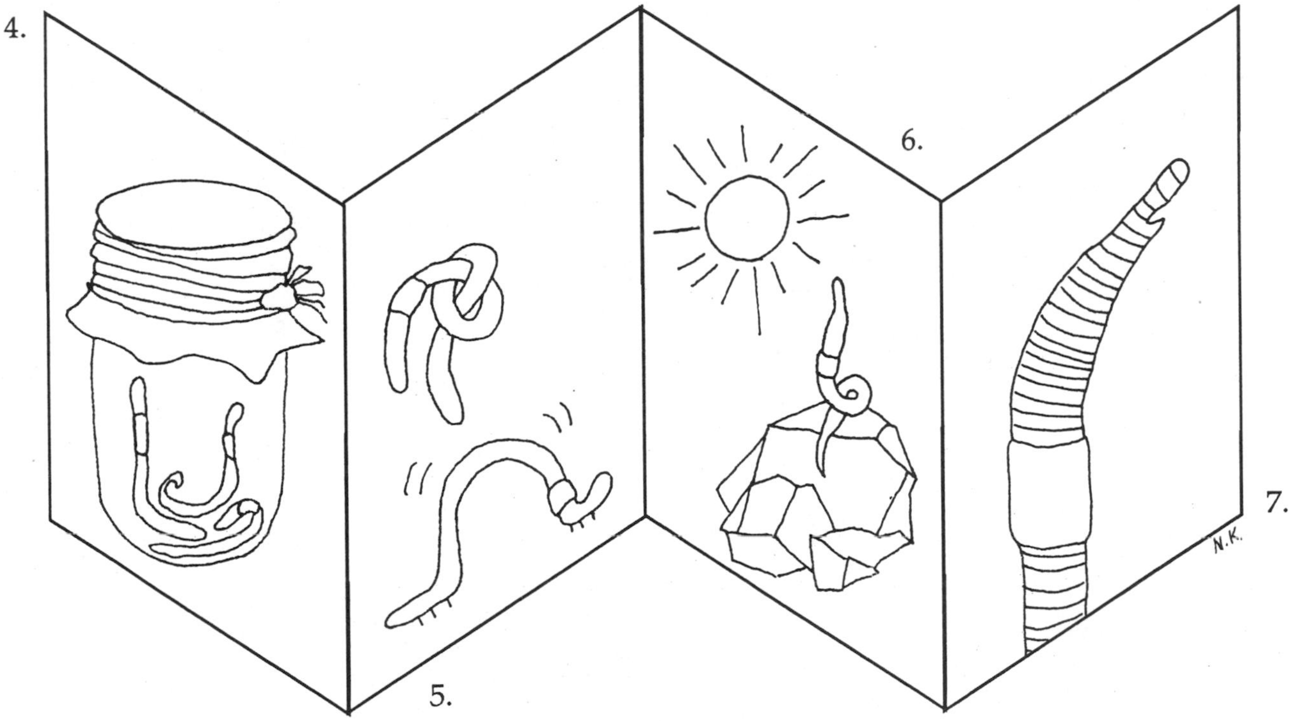

1.

3.

2.

4.

6.

5.

7.

N.K.

Bonus Activity   Write a sentence describing what's wrong in each picture.

Name_____ **Worm-Blooded**

One way to classify animals is by body temperature. Birds and mammals are warm-blooded because they have a constant natural body heat. Each species has its own specific temperature. Cold-blooded animals have blood that varies in temperature depending upon the surrounding air, land, or water. Fishes and reptiles are cold-blooded animals.

Wormformation

Directions

Classify the following animals by writing the name of each in the correct category.

Texas Horned Lizard

_____
ANIMALS
_____

__ turtle	__ Texas horned lizard	__ bird
__ lion	__ trout	__ human
__ horse	__ kangaroo	__ cat
__ snake	__ raccoon	__ frog
__ snail	__ fish	__ earthworm

Coral Snake

COLD-BLOODED	WARM-BLOODED

Bonus Activity Select one cold-blooded and one warm-blooded animal to research. Write a description that includes where it lives, what it eats, what its needs are, and what it looks like.

Warm or Cold

Killer Whale

Gecko

Opossum

Directions
Classify the following animals by writing the name of each in the correct category.
You may need to use reference books to identify some of these more unusual animals.

ANIMALS

__ lemming	__ starling	__ shrike
__ woodchuck	__ sturgeon	__ seal
__ iguana	__ gunnel	__ gazelle
__ pipit	__ fisher	__ alligator
__ opossum	__ skink	__ skunk
__ killer whale	__ ermine	__ cottonmouth
__ gecko	__ egret	__ cobra

COLD-BLOODED	WARM-BLOODED

Bonus Activity What is the normal body temperature of a human being? What is a cat's normal temperature? How can you tell the temperature of an earthworm?

> Worms are good food for many animals because worms are high in protein. Like humans, other animals need to eat protein to survive. A fat, juicy worm is to a bird as a thick, juicy steak is to a human.
> **Wormformation**

Earthworm Casting

Directions

Complete these analogies. Write the word or words that belong in each empty space. (*Hint: To create an analogy means to explain something by comparing it with something else.*)

1. A worm is to a bird as a steak is to a_____.

2. A worm bin is to a worm as a barn is to a _____.

3. A tunnel is to a muskrat as a burrow is to a_____.

4. Castings are to worms as manure is to _____.

5. Teeth are to a human as a _____ is to a bird.

6. Lungs are to mammals as _____ is to worms.

7. Scales are to a reptile as _____ are to a bird.

8. Warm-blooded is to mammals as _____ is to reptiles.

9. Potting soil is to a plant as_____ is to a worm.

10. A hatchling is to a worm as a baby _____ is to a hen.

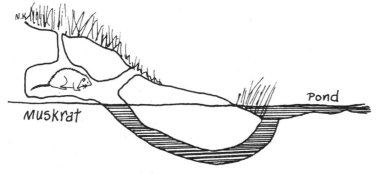

Pond

Muskrat

Bonus Activity
Write analogies for a friend to complete.

Worms as Food

Earthworms are important members of the food web. They serve as food for many kinds of animals. For example, moles tunnel through the soil in search of earthworms. The moles catch worms and place them in a storage area for later consumption. To keep a worm from escaping, the mole may bite off its first three to five anterior segments.

Scientific records may be misleading about whether or not earthworms make up a part of an animal's diet. To find out what an animal eats, biologists look at stomach contents and feces. Because worms are soft-bodied and have no bones, few undigested remains are left to examine. Careful examination of a sample under a microscope, however, may show earthworm setae. Because setae are made of tough, durable, chitin, they may not be digested. (Insect bodies are also made of chitin.) Biologists may misinterpret what an animal actually eats if they do not think to look for setae.

Wormformation

Directions

Use references; read the Wormformation. Circle each animal that you think might eat live earthworms as part of its diet.

N.K. Mole

N.K. Centipede

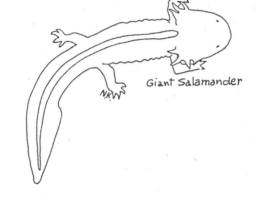
N.K. Giant Salamander

N.K Water Shrew

Leopard Frog N.K.

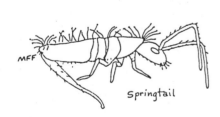
MFF Springtail

Green Snake N.K.

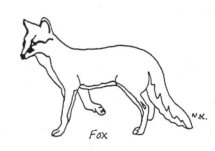
Fox N.K.

N.K. Sow Bug

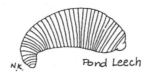
Pond Leech N.K.

MFF Fruit Fly

Animals are not drawn to scale.

Wormformation

A bird which eats earthworms is the woodcock. Baby woodcocks eat only earthworms. When the ground freezes too severely, the young birds cannot find earthworms to eat. In northern climates where they live, the ground may freeze very hard and deep in winter. Some earthworms keep from dying by tunneling deep in the earth before it freezes solid. During these very cold winters, the woodcock population decreases dramatically because the young birds do not survive to become adults.

Directions

Use references and read the Wormformation. Circle each animal that you think might eat live earthworms as part of its diet.

Animals are not drawn to scale.

A worm eats the leaf. A fish eats the worm. A bird eats the fish. A cat eats the bird. This sequence of who feeds on whom is called a food chain. Through observation, biologists learn these relationships. They often create diagrams to help them understand the correct order. By applying knowledge of the food chains, scientists can learn what animals are affected by pollution or what waters are polluted.

Wormformation

Directions

Cut out the organisms pictured in boxes below. Paste them in the correct order to form three food chains. There is more than one right answer. If the organism you want to use is not labeled, write it in a blank box. Always start with a part of a plant in the first link. Fill as many links as you can. (*Hint: Organisms can be used in more than one food chain.*)

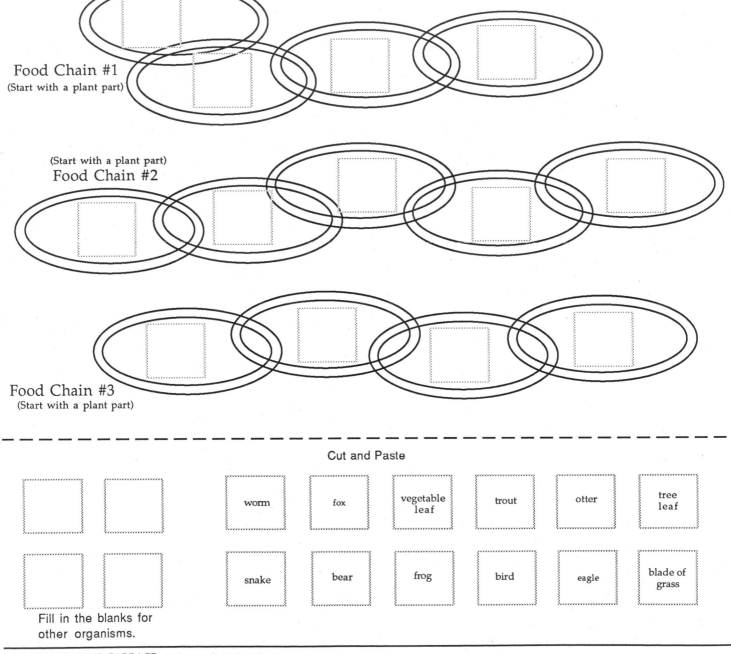

Food Chain #1
(Start with a plant part)

(Start with a plant part)
Food Chain #2

Food Chain #3
(Start with a plant part)

- -

Cut and Paste

		worm	fox	vegetable leaf	trout	otter	tree leaf
		snake	bear	frog	bird	eagle	blade of grass

Fill in the blanks for other organisms.

WORMS EAT OUR GARBAGE Copyright © 1993 Flower Press

Comprehension

Rachel Carson was a biologist who used her skill at writing to change people's lives. She wrote the book **Silent Spring** in 1962. In it, she explained how certain chemicals manufactured in industrial laboratories could threaten life on our earth.

Farmers used one such chemical, DDT, to save crops by killing the insects which destroyed the crop. Rachel Carson pointed out that DDT and other pesticides (pest killers) killed not only harmful insects, but also good ones. Through the food chain, birds, fish, and small mammals also died.

A bird may eat hundreds of insects, each containing a small amount of pesticide. The amount of pesticide in one insect may not be enough to kill the bird, but small doses multiplied many times can. Or, if a fox eats a bird weakened by harmful chemicals, the life of the fox is threatened.

The sounds of spring--bird songs, the scurrying of the animals, the coming alive of nature after a long winter--were welcome sounds to Rachel Carson. She could not tolerate the prospect of springtimes made silent by the presence of unseen chemicals distributed throughout the environment with little caution. Her story is one of scholarship, dedication, commitment, and courage.

Wormformation

Directions
Using reference materials and **Wormformation** answer the questions below.

1. What is a food chain?_____

_____

2. Rachel Carson was a biologist. What do biologists study?_____

_____

3. In 1962, what chemical did many farmers use to destroy pests on their crops?

_____

4. Why do you think Rachel Carson titled her book **Silent Spring?**_____

_____

5. How does the use of chemical pesticides threaten the health of people?

_____

_____

Bonus Activity Read more about Rachel Carson. Share your information with a friend.

Comprehension

Wormformation

The difference between fact and opinion is what can be proven or not proven. For example, it is a fact that worms have lived up to 3 years in captivity. Someone has observed this to be true. But if a person says, "Worms are my friends," it is his opinion because it can't be proven.

Directions

Read the *Wormformation* box. Answer which is fact and which is opinion in statements #1 through #6. Place an **X** in the correct box.

Fact ☐ or Opinion ☐

1. Earthworms hide from the light.

Fact ☐ or Opinion ☐ 2. Everyone likes worms.

3. All earthworms have red blood. Fact ☐ or Opinion ☐

4. Worms feel vibrations in the ground. Fact ☐ or Opinion ☐

6. Earthworms are a gardener's best friend.
Fact ☐ or Opinion ☐

5. Redworms can be found in piles of horse manure.

Fact ☐ or Opinion ☐

7. Worms are slimy.
Fact ☐ or Opinion ☐

N.K.

WORMS EAT OUR GARBAGE Copyright © 1993 Flower Press

Comprehension

- Some people say a nightcrawler lives in <u>dirt</u>, but it is better to call its environment <u>soil</u>.
- Desert sand or a climate with little rain is not a good environment for an earthworm, but a humus-rich, wet garden is.
- A worm may hide in its burrow close to the entrance where a hungry raccoon, robin, turtle, or snake can catch and eat it.
- A fox can listen for worms by cocking its ears toward the ground. With a quick pounce, the fox catches a nutritious worm meal.
- A redworm can be found in a compost pile made of leaves and other organic material such as garden and grass trimmings. **Wormformation**

Directions

Complete the crossword puzzle. The word clues are listed below. One of the words is given to help you get started.

Hints: 1) All of the word answers can be found in Wormformation.
2) When two words cross they share the same letter.

Across
1. shelled reptile
4. "masked" animal
7. red wriggler
9. earth
11. vegetable habitat
12. moist
13. leap _____
14. legless reptile

Down
2. water from sky
3. quick as a _____
5. decayed organics
6. dew worm
7. red-breasted bird
8. grain of _____
10. tree food factories

Name_____

My Worm Story

Directions
Use your imagination. Read this
story and write in the missing words.

I have a favorite worm. Its name is _____.

It is _____ inches long and has _____ skin color.

My worm lives in the_____.

Its favorite foods are_____.

If my worm could talk, it would say, "_____

_____

_____."

If my worm could play a game, the game would be _____

_____.

If my worm could take a vacation, it would go to _____

_____.

If my worm could watch a television show, it would watch

_____.

If my worm could describe me, it would say, "My friend_____

_____

_____.

I love my worm because _____

_____

_____.

Bonus Activity Give three reasons why you love your worm.

WORMS EAT OUR GARBAGE Copyright © 1993 Flower Press

Creativity

Directions
Read each sentence and write the missing word in the boxes to the right. The one-word answers are partly filled in for you.

1. The opposite of cold-blooded is _____ blooded.   w Ⓞ r ☐

2. Nightcrawlers eat _____.   l e ⓐ ☐ Ⓞ s

3. All worms need _____.   m o ☐ s t ☐ ⓡ ☐

4. Bristles that help a worm move are called _____.   s ☐ t ☐ e

5. A worm's swollen band is a _____.   Ⓒ ☐ i t e ☐ l ☐ m

6. The mouth of a worm is at its_____end.   a ☐ ⓣ e r ☐ Ⓞ o ☐

7. Red is the color of a worm's _____.   ⓑ l ☐ ☐ d

Bonus Activity   Unscramble the letters that are circled to find the name of very small organisms that worms eat.

Unscrambled word_____

An earthworm feels slimy because it has glands in the skin that give off mucus. The mucus keeps the earthworm's body moist. For the body to stay moist, the earthworm needs damp surroundings.   **Wormformation**

Directions

Answer the questions. Place an X over yes or no. Provide reasons for your answers.

Where would you most likely find a healthy worm?

Reason Why

- in a dry garden?

  | Yes | No | _____

- in the sunlight?

  | Yes | No | _____

- in a burrow?

  | Yes | No | _____

- under a rock?

  | Yes | No | _____

- in a shady flower bed?

  | Yes | No | _____

- on a sandy beach?

  | Yes | No | _____

Bonus Activity Write a paragraph describing where you would most likely find a worm in your neighborhood.

Worms at Work

Learner Outcomes

After completing the activities in this unit, the student will:

- be able to set up a worm bin

- be able to maintain a worm bin

- understand the work of worms and their companions in and out of the bin

- understand the process of vermicomposting

- understand the concept of "living soil"

- understand relationships between worms and plants

- be able to make and test hypotheses

- be able to record observations, interpret data, and arrive at conclusions

The Worm Who Came to Dinner

by Mary Frances Fenton

Sara was both happy and sad. Yesterday was the last day of school. Although she was happy to be on vacation, she would miss her friends. Also, it was hard for Sara to admit to herself that she would miss learning the new things she found out about in school. Sara did look forward to visiting her Grandmother's, because Grandmother always had something interesting going on in her home.

(At Grandmother's)   As Sara helped Grandmother fix supper, she asked, "Where do you want me to put these apple peels?"

Grandmother replied, "Put them right in this bowl for now. Later, you can help me feed them to the worms."

"Worms? What do you mean, feed them to the worms?" asked Sara in disbelief.

"Well, my dear, I've got a new way to get rid of my garbage. I feed it to worms, and they turn it into potting soil for my garden," answered Grandmother. "And we have worms for fishing."

Well, Sara didn't know whether she liked the whole idea, or not. But it was all so new to her, it intrigued her. So, she followed Grandmother when she went to feed the worms the kitchen food scraps. She got to see for herself how one could keep a number of worms in captivity. After a few visits that summer, Sara was able to feed them and learn to respect them as good little workers.

Now, Sara found that Grandmother kept a box down in the basement--in a corner where it was kind of dark. There was, however, a light you could turn on so that you could see. The box was just a plain old wooden one that Grandfather had around. They drilled holes in the box so air could come in. Sara learned that worms had to have air to live.

There was a plastic cover on top of the box of worms. It laid loosely like a blanket--it wasn't sealed tightly so worms could have air from the top, as well as in or near the bottom.

Grandmother peeled back the cover. Sara looked in expecting to see scads of worms squirming around on the top of the box, and . . . she didn't see anything! All she saw was what looked like black dirt.

"Where are the worms?" Sara asked.

Grandmother chuckled, "Well, they're down in the bedding. They don't like light, so they quickly moved away and down into the bedding when I took the cover off. That's where they live and work, down in that damp bedding."

Then, Grandmother plunged her hand down into the box, into the bedding, and down deep under the surface. She pulled up a handful of stuff and turned it over and--sure enough--there were the worms, all wiggling and glistening in the dim light of the basement.

Seeing the surprise on Sara's face, Grandmother said, "I happen to know where I buried the last batch of table scraps. I want to make sure that I don't stick my hand down where the last pile of garbage was buried. I keep a chart. That way I know where I've buried what, so I don't have to put my hand in the last two night's garbage."

Sara thought, "That's a good idea. I wouldn't handle it when it's decomposing--it stinks!"

Grandmother said, "Now, here's a handful of compost without garbage in it. Smell my hands." Sara didn't really want to, but Grandmother said, "See, it doesn't smell bad."

"No--it doesn't smell bad," mumbled Sara. "It smells like dirt."

"Well, yes, it does smell like organic humus," Grandmother went on to say.

Sara didn't know what humus meant, but she didn't ask the question about what that was at this moment. She was more interested in the worms squiggling around in Grandmother's hand. Her grandmother put the worms back, saying, "We'll put them back so they can go back to work. They don't like to be out in the air, because their bodies have to be moist."

Sara said, "Oh. I guess that's why you see them crawling around in the rain, then. You don't see worms on sunny days, you see them when it rains."

"That's right. Very good," Grandmother replied. "So when I check the box every couple of days or so, I make sure that there is enough moisture. I either put my hand in, or use a fork or something to make sure that the worms are kept happy. The worms will stay right here in the box if everything is here that they need."

Sara said, "You mean they never crawl out?"

Grandmother replied, "No, for the reason you just gave, that they don't like dry places. They're not going to crawl where it's dry. It's only wet and moist in the box."

"Oh, yes, that's right," thought Sara. Then she asked, "How much garbage can you bury in here, Grandmother?"

"Well," Grandmother said, "When it's just Grandfather and me here, and not you and your mother and father visiting me, we can probably bury 4 pounds of garbage a week. But, when I have lots of company, then I have too much garbage for the worms."

At this, Sara looked surprised. Her eyes got big, and she asked, "You mean you can feed them too much?"

Grandmother said, "Yes, you can."

"Oh, then what do you do with the extra garbage?" asked Sara. Grandmother replied, "Well, that can be a problem, but there are a number of ways we can solve that."

WORMS EAT OUR GARBAGE Copyright © 1993 Flower Press   Reading Comprehension

Sara was confident that Grandmother knew what she was doing, so she didn't ask any more questions about the extra garbage. She asked, "Can I hold one of the worms?"

"Of course. Here, let's try this corner," Grandmother said as she peeled back some bedding that was made of shredded newspaper. "I'll peel this back, because I know there's no garbage buried in this corner. See if you can find a worm down there."

Sara said, "Oh, there's one! There's a worm!" Sara picked it up and put it in her hand. She watched it twist and turn and sort of look like it was looking for a place to go, as if it didn't know where it was in her hand. This was a new place for it; it didn't want to be there exactly, so it was trying to move away.

She noted that one end of the worm was definitely the end that wanted to move in some direction. It was waving around, trying to figure out which direction to go.   Sara said, "Grand-mother, does the worm have a head and a tail? I know it has a tail, but I don't see a head. The head end looks like a tail."

Grandmother said, "That's true. We don't have a microscope, or a magnifying glass, but if we did, you could see that there is a difference between one end and the other, even though they both look 'pointy.' Do you see that swollen band close to one end?"

Sara said, "Yes. What is it?"

"That's called a clitellum," Grandmother replied. "That is a part of their reproductive system. That helps them develop cocoons so that baby worms can hatch from them."

Sara thought, "Baby worms? Cocoons? What was all that?"

Grandmother continued, "We'll talk more about that later. Right now, look at the way it moves. I want you to touch it. Does it feel slimy to you?"

"No. It just kind of tickles my hand," Sara said.

And Grandmother said, "A lot of people think worms are slimy, but they're really not. They are a little bit moist, but they're not slimy like snails."

"Yeah, snails are particularly slimy," Sara agreed. She put the worm back and covered it back up with bedding, knowing that it didn't like being away from its moist home.

Sara was pleased that she learned something new. She thought it was great that her grandparents knew special things and shared them with her.

Sara joked with her grandmother, "The next time I come, do you think we could bake a treat for the *worm who came to dinner*?"

The End

WORMS EAT OUR GARBAGE Copyright © 1993 Flower Press   Reading Compredhesion

Name_____ **Story Memories**

Directions
Read the story, *The Worm Who Came to Dinner*. Write the missing words in each sentence.

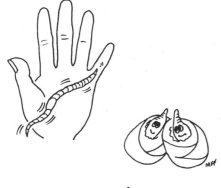

1. From this story you learned that worm bedding is made

   of_____ .

2. Grandmother uses a_____ to keep track

   of where she buried the garbage.

3. You can see worms crawling on the sidewalk on a

   _____ morning.

4. The swollen band around a worm's body

   is called a_____.

5. A baby worm hatches from a _____.

6. Worms stay deep in the bedding to keep their bodies

   _____ and to avoid exposure

   to_____.

7. Grandmother feeds her worms _____

   _____.

8. Grandmother keeps her worms in a _____
   room.

9. Another use for Grandmother's worms besides eating her

   garbage is _____.

Bonus Activity What do you think will happen the next time Sara goes to visit her grandparents?
Write your story.

WORMS EAT OUR GARBAGE Copyright © 1993 Flower Press

Reading Comprehension

Directions
Draw a picture of your favorite part of the story *The Worm Who Came to Dinner*, page 56-58.

_____
Write a title for the picture here.

Directions

This is a checklist to follow when creating your worm bin. Check each step when completed and make comments about your observations and feelings.

☐ *Worm Bin Checklist* ☐

☐ 1. Weigh food waste for two to three weeks to get the average amount of garbage produced.

_____

_____

☐ 2. Select size of worm bin needed and purchase or build it.

_____

_____

☐ 3. Determine amount of worms you need.

_____

_____

☐ 4. Mail order or collect the worms. (Allow 4-6 weeks for delivery of worms.)

_____

_____

☐ 5. Prepare the correct volume of newspaper bedding and place in worm bin before the worms arrive._____

_____

☐ 6. Mix a small amount of soil with the bedding in worm bin.

_____

_____

☐ 7. Add worms to bedding.

_____

_____

☐ 8. Bury garbage.

_____

_____

☐ 9. Maintain worm bin moisture.

_____

_____

☐ 10. Observe worms, cocoons, and other organisms in the worm bin frequently.

_____

_____

☐ 11. When the worm bin is full of castings, remove castings, and replace with new bedding.

_____

_____

☐ 12. Use castings, vermicompost, or castings tea on your plants.

_____

_____

Directions

Millie got all mixed up in creating her worm bin. The steps below are in the wrong order.
Help Millie. Write the sentences in the most logical order on the lower half of the page.
(*Hint: Write the correct number in each box. The first one is done for you.*)

[1.] Determine the size of the worm bin.

[ ] Add worms to worm bin.

[ ] Harvest castings to feed your plants.

[ ] Bury garbage in the bedding.

[ ] Put bedding in the worm bin.

[ ] Build the worm bin.

[ ] Replace castings with fresh bedding.

**Steps in
Setting Up
a Worm Bin**

1. _____
   _____
2. _____
   _____
3. _____
   _____
4. _____
   _____
5. _____
   _____
6. _____
   _____
7. _____
   _____

Name_____ # Worm Food in Your Trash

Wormformation
You can raise redworms to eat some of your own organic waste. You need to provide a proper container, damp bedding, and food scraps. The worms will eat the food scraps as well as the small, microscopic organisms which also help decompose the food.

Directions

Here is a list of things people often throw in their trash can. Which of these could be fed to worms in a worm bin? Circle your answers.

rice

newspaper

carrot tops

broccoli stalk

grapefruit rind

onion skin

watermelon rind

plate scrapings

plastic bag

bread crust

celery

tin can

junk mail

glass jar

chicken bone

rubber band

apple core

cheese

Bonus Activity Make a list of worm food most likely to be found in the trash can at <u>your</u> home.

WORMS EAT OUR GARBAGE Copyright © 1993 Flower Press

Discrimination

Directions

Write the names of things a worm will likely eat if they are put them in the worm bin. List one for each letter of the alphabet. Brand names of things can be used. The first one is done for you.

A **Asparagus** _____

B _____

C _____

D _____

E _____

F _____

G _____

H _____

I _____

J _____

K _____

L _____

M _____

N _____

O _____

P _____

Q _____

R _____

S _____

T _____

U _____

V _____

W _____

X _____

Y _____

Z _____

> How much garbage can worms eat? A worm can consume about one-half of its weight each day. A worm weighing 1 gram (1 g) might eat 1/2 g of food in one day. Or, 1 pound (1 lb) of worms could eat 1/2 lb of garbage each day. It makes little difference if the pound of worms is made up of 600 big worms, or 1500 small worms. When redworms eat garbage, the garbage disappears at about the same rate depending upon the weight, or mass of the worms. **Wormformation**

Materials
- 2-quart plastic pail
- weighing balance or scale

Directions

Collect food waste in a plastic pail. Weigh it on a scale. Use the chart to keep track of how many ounces of organic food waste your class produces each week at lunchtime. Answer the questions below. *(Hint: Subtract the weight of the pail from the weight of the food waste.)*

	Week 1	Week 2	Week 3
Monday			
Tuesday			
Wednesday			
Thursday			
Friday			

Total Ounces per Week: _____ oz   _____ oz   _____ oz

1. Average Ounces per Week: oz per   oz per   oz per

$$\frac{\text{Week 1} + \text{Week 2} + \text{Week 3}}{3 \text{ weeks}} = \underline{\hspace{2cm}} \text{ average oz garbage per week}$$

2. Average Ounces per Day:

$$\frac{\text{average oz garbage per week}}{7 \text{ days per week}} = \underline{\hspace{2cm}} \text{ average oz garbage per day}$$

3. To find out how many worms you need to start your worm bin, do the following equation. *(Hint: It takes twice the weight of worms to consume a given amount of garbage.)*

$$\text{average oz garbage per day} \quad \times \quad 2 \quad = \quad \underline{\hspace{3cm}}$$

4. Convert from ounces to pounds the *average oz garbage per day* and the weight of worms needed to process that amount of garbage.

   a. average oz garbage per day $\dfrac{\underline{\hspace{2cm}}}{16 \text{ oz per lb}}$ = $\underline{\hspace{2cm}}$

   b. oz worms $\dfrac{\underline{\hspace{2cm}}}{16 \text{ oz per lb}}$ = $\underline{\hspace{2cm}}$

Bonus Activity
List the kinds of food that were wasted. Give your opinion as to why they were wasted.

The Big Paper Shredding Event

1. Open the newspaper to the centerfold.

2. Tear it lengthwise down the centerfold.

3. Gather the two halves.

4. Tear them lengthwise again.

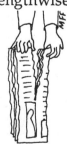

5. Repeat process four or more times until you have long shreds from 1 to 3 inches wide.

Wormformation

To make a proper home for your worms, you will need worm bedding. Newspaper makes a good bedding. Shred it, moisten it, and place it in your worm bin. It has four main purposes:

- Bedding holds moisture for the worms.
- Bedding gives the worms a medium in which to live.
- Bedding makes air available to worms anywhere in the bin.
- Bedding gives you material to cover the garbage you bury.

Worms also eat their bedding, but it does not have much food value for them.

Materials Needed

- 1' x 2' x 3' worm bin (approximate size)
- large plastic bag
- 10 lb newspaper (no colored pages or slick paper)
- 1 cup soil (grit for worms' gizzards)
- water

Directions

Make up the bedding for your worm bin by following steps 1-6.

6. Place shreds in plastic bag to store or place in worm bin. Add water.

(Hint: Tear with the grain of the paper. If you cannot tear long strips, then you are probably tearing against the grain. You need to turn the paper 90° before tearing it.)

Bonus Activity How else can you use shredded or unshredded newspaper? Make a list.

Name_____   # Worm/Garbage Ratio

Wormformation

Worms can eat only <u>so</u> much garbage. How many worms can consume how much garbage? The relationship between the weight of worms required to process a given amount of garbage is called the "worm to garbage" ratio. A worm : garbage ratio of 2:1 is just about right. That is, it takes 2 pounds of redworms to process an average of one pound of garbage per day.

Directions
Read the Wormformation. Solve the math problems below using this ratio:

Worms : Garbage = 2 : 1

Circle the best answer for each question.

We <u>do</u> have limits!

1. George lives in an apartment by himself. He averages 4 oz of kitchen waste per day. How many redworms will he need to set up his worm bin?

   a. 4 oz worms   b. 8 oz worms   c. 16 oz worms   d. 24 oz worms

2. Elin, Kathy, and Elin's two children live in a house with a small vegetable garden in the back. Both adults are vegetarians. The household averages 1 lb of food waste per day. How many worms will they need to start up a worm bin?

   a. 1/2 lb worms   b. 1 1/2 lb worms   c. 2 lb worms   d. 1/4 lb worms

3. Mr. Taylor's class measured its food waste for 3 weeks and found that they produced 100 oz of garbage per week, or an average of 20 oz per day. How many worms will they need to start up a worm bin in the classroom?

   a. 400 oz worms   b. 200 oz worms   c. 80 oz worms   d. 40 oz worms

4. Twenty adult neighbors on Green Street came together and built a common worm bin. They located it in the middle of the block in Laticia's backyard. They produced an average of 80 oz of garbage each day. How many <u>pounds</u> of worms will they need to set up the neighborhood worm bin? *(Hint: There are 16 oz in a pound.)* (_____oz ÷ 16 oz = _____ lb)

   a. 3 lb worms   b. 80 oz worms   c. 10 lb worms   d. 1 1/2 lb worms

Bonus Activity
   Camp Meadowlark staff set up a worm bin near the kitchen. Thirty campers and staff ate meals everyday thoughout the summer. Each person produced about 4 oz of food waste per day. If they set up a worm bin with 7.5 lb worms, will this amount be enough to process the amount of waste produced daily?
                    Yes ___ No ___
                    If No, then how many lb of worms do they need?_____

   There are about 1,000 redworms in a pound. How many worms would it take to set up Camp Meadowlark's worm bin? _____

A ratio shows that there is a fixed relationship between two things. A ratio can be expressed in words, as in "a three to one ratio." A ratio can also be expressed with symbols, as in ■■■:□. Usually, a combination of numbers and a symbol is used to express a ratio, as in a 3:1 ratio or 1:3 ratio. The symbol ":" means "to."

Wormformation

Directions

Use **Wormformation** to help you answer the following questions.

1. What ratio does the following series of symbols represent?

   □ □ □ : ■   _____ 3 : _____

2. For every three apples, there are how many pears?

      _____

3. Give the ratio illustrated by this:

   _____

4. For each ⬭ , how many ⟋ are there in problem 3?

   _____

5. There are four sow bugs for every centipede in your worm bin. Draw a picture below expressing this ratio in symbols.

6. How would you express the ratio given in problem 5 in words?

   _____

7. How would you express the ratio in problem 5 in numbers and symbols?

   _____

8. Can a ratio be expressed this way, 1:2? That is, can the smaller number appear first?   _____ Yes   _____ No

Worms in a worm bin do not have to be fed every day. However, it is important to know the average amount of food waste you can feed your worms. If you produce 7 pounds of garbage in one week, that would be an average of one pound of garbage per day. One way to show this is:

$$\frac{7 \text{ lb garbage per week}}{7 \text{ days in one week}} = 1 \text{ lb garbage per day average}$$

Wormformation

We eat leftover leftovers on the weekend!

Directions

Using **Wormformation** as a guide, answer the following questions to practice finding average amounts of garbage produced per day:

1. If you measured 14 lb of garbage per week, what was the average amount of garbage produced per day?

$$\frac{14 \text{ lb garbage per week}}{7 \text{ days in one week}} = \text{_____} \text{lb garbage per day average}$$

2. Suzie and Ross measured 3.5 lb garbage per week at home. What was the average amount of garbage their family produced per day?

$$\frac{3.5 \text{ lb garbage per week}}{7 \text{ days in one week}} = \text{_____} \text{lb garbage per day average}$$

3. Wild Bill's food coop was considering using a worm bin to process the waste from its produce. Pete found that they produced about 50 pounds of food waste in 10 days. What was the average amount of garbage produced per day?

$$\frac{50 \text{ lb garbage per 10 days}}{10 \text{ days}} = \text{_____} \text{lb garbage per day average}$$

4. Mrs. Smith's class measured its lunchroom food waste for 3 weeks. They had an average of 300 ounces of garbage during the 5 day week. What was the average amount of food waste produced each day?

$$\frac{\text{_____ oz garbage per 5 days}}{5 \text{ days}} = \text{_____} \text{oz garbage per day average}$$

5. Mr. Taylor's class also measured its food waste for 3 weeks. They averaged 200 oz of garbage during the 5-day week. Writing your own equation, calculate the average amount of food waste produced per day. Be sure to label your answers!

_____ = _____

Bonus Activity

Calculate the amount of kitchen waste your family produces each day.

Wormformation

Worms require a certain amount of space (volume) to work in to process garbage. A rule of thumb is to set up a worm bin with about 1/4 pound of worms for every cubic foot. The ideal worm bin is quite shallow, usually no more than one foot deep. The reason for shallow worm bins with large surface area is to allow more air to contact the bedding. It does not matter whether the bin is square, rectangular, or round, as long as it is not much more than one foot deep.

Directions

This chart shows how big a worm bin should be to handle different amounts of garbage. Each worm bin in the chart is one foot deep. Use the chart to answer the questions below.

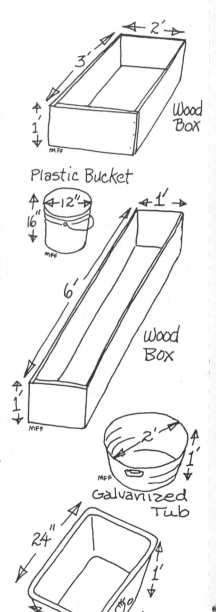

Worm Bin Number	Food waste per day A	Initial weight of worms B (A×2=B)	Surface area of worm bin C (B×4=C)	Food waste per week D (A × 7 days = D)
1	0.25 lb	0.5 lb	2 sq ft	1.75 lb
2	0.5 lb	1.0 lb	4 sq ft	3.5 lb
3	1.0 lb	2.0 lb	8 sq ft	7.0 lb
4	1.5 lb	3.0 lb	12 sq ft	10.5 lb
5	2.0 lb	4.0 lb	16 sq ft	14.0 lb
6	3.0 lb	6.0 lb	24 sq ft	21.0 lb
7	4.0 lb	8.0 lb	32 sq ft	28.0 lb

1. How many pounds of worms will you need to set up a worm bin if the amount of food waste produced per day is 1.5 lb?

   _____

2. How many square feet of surface area are needed to provide a home for 3 lb worms and 1.5 lb food waste per day?

   _____

3. How many pounds of food waste can a worm bin handle per week if it has 4 sq ft of surface area?

   _____

4. If you had a worm bin that was 16 sq ft in surface area, how many pounds of garbage could it handle per week?

   _____

Bonus Activity Calculate the length and width of a worm bin to give it a surface area of 12 sq ft.

Wormformation

A worm's body consists of about 75% to 90% water. Its surface must be moist in order for the worm to respire (to exchange the gases oxygen and carbon dioxide). When you prepare bedding with about the same moisture content (75%) as the worm's body, the worm's home will not be too dry or too wet. It will be just right.

Directions

Read the Wormformation and complete the following steps to find how much material you need to prepare your worms' bedding.

1. Measure the length, width and height of your worm bin.

    length _____ inches
    width   _____ inches
    height _____ inches

2. Multiply these worm bin dimensions to get the number of cubic inches.
   (*Hint: Cubic inches or feet are a measurement of volume.*)

   _____ inches X _____ inches X _____ inches = _____ cubic inches
   length   width   height

3. Calculate how many cubic feet in your worm bin by dividing the number of cubic inches by 1,728 (the number of cubic inches in one cubic foot).

   _____ cubic inches ÷ __1,728__ cubic inches = _____ cubic feet in
                             per cubic foot   worm bin

4. You will need 2.5 pounds of shredded newspaper for every cubic foot in your worm bin. How many pounds will you need?

   _____ pounds of newspaper

5. To figure how much water you must add to the shredded newspaper to make the worm bedding 75% moist, multiply the 3 pounds of the newspaper needed by three (3). How many pounds of water will you need?

   _____ pounds of water

Bonus Activity Complete the five steps above for each of the following worm bins:
* wooden worm bin (1 foot by 2 feet by 3 feet)
* *Worm-a-way*® worm bin (20 inches by 24 inches by 12 inches)
* patio bench worm bin (12 inches by 24 inches by 42 inches)

Wormformation

The day the worms come you will want to put them their new home and feed them. Before you place them in the bin, you can use the worms to make several observations. When you complete your observations, spread the worms on top of the bedding in their new home. Dig a hole in the bedding big enough to contain the food waste you saved. Place the garbage in the hole and spread some bedding over it. Your worms are now in their new home. If you take care of them, they will grow and reproduce. Some worms may live as long as four years in a worm bin.

Directions

Read the Wormformation and complete the following observations.

Materials

- 1 lb of redworms in their shipping container
- worm bin set up with properly moistened bedding
- stopwatch, digital watch or watch with second hands
- 1/2 lb of food waste to feed the worms
- cardboard
- plastic sheet or newpaper (covering for table)

Observations

1. Place a sheet of plastic or a newspaper on a table. Open the container of worms and dump its contents on the table. Time how long it takes for the worms to disappear into the bedding.

How long did it take for the worms to disappear?_____

Describe what you observed._____

2. Gently bring the worms to the surface again. Be careful so you do not injure their soft bodies. Observe how long it takes worms "in the shade" to disappear and how long it takes worms "in the light" to disappear. Hold a piece of cardboard over part of the pile of worms to shade that portion of the worms from the light. Time how long it takes both groups of worms to disappear into the bedding.

How long did it take for the worms in the shade to disappear?_____

How long did it take for the worms in the light to disappear?_____

Compare these times with the first observations you made._____

What can you tell about the worms from these observations?_____

_____

_____

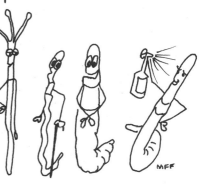

Wormformation
The length of an earthworm depends upon several factors:
- What kind of worm it is
- How old it is
- How well-fed it is
- Whether its body has enough moisture

Materials
- moist paper towel
- ruler with metric and inch scales
- toothpick
- shallow dish of water
- small tray
- 1 live worm

Introduction
If you have observed a worm carefully, you know that even a well-fed, adult worm whose skin is glistening with moisture can vary in length. When a worm stretches out, it is long and skinny. When a worm contracts, or squeezes up, it is shorter and thicker. Measuring the length of a worm can be a challenge. With practice and a cooperative worm, you should be able to get a reasonably accurate measurement which you can share with your class.

Directions
Slightly moisten a paper towel. Get a worm from its container and rinse it off in the dish of water. Place your toothpick under your worm in the water and transfer it to the moist paper towel.

To measure your worm, use the toothpick to guide the worm into a straight line. Then, quickly mark the moist towel at the anterior end and posterior end of the worm. Measure the distance between the two points and record your figures on the chart below. Repeat this technique for the other measurements.

	Length in Inches	Length in Centimeters	Width in Inches	Width in Centimeters
Stretched out				
Contracted				
Sum				
Divided by 2				
Average				

Bonus Activity Measure more worms. Make a graph of the results.

Once someone goes to the effort of measuring large numbers of objects, how do they talk about what they found? How can they present their findings so that others will know what they discovered? One way is to make a graph of the numbers in an easy-to-read form. One such chart is a histogram, or bar graph. It is a series of blocks of different heights to compare different sets of measurements.

Wormformation

Directions

Tangi, Lakisha, and Nate each measured the lengths of seven redworms with a metric ruler. The results are below. Place a mark in the correct size range on the Tally Chart for each length. Make a histogram. Answer the questions that follow. (*Hint: The first size range is done for you.*)

Tangi

Redworm	Length
1.	1.5 cm
2.	2.5 cm
3.	3.0 cm
4.	4.5 cm
5.	8.0 cm
6.	7.5 cm
7.	6.0 cm

Lakisha

Redworm	Length
1.	4.5 cm
2.	9.0 cm
3.	3.0 cm
4.	2.5 cm
5.	8.5 cm
6.	2.0 cm
7.	10.0 cm

Nate

Redworm	Length
1.	2.5 cm
2.	3.5 cm
3.	9.5 cm
4.	1.5 cm
5.	6.5 cm
6.	5.5 cm
7.	3.5 cm

Tally Chart

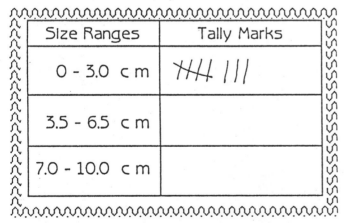

Size Ranges	Tally Marks
0 – 3.0 c m	ⵞⵞ |||
3.5 – 6.5 c m	
7.0 – 10.0 c m	

Total Numbers and Lengths of Redworms by Size Range

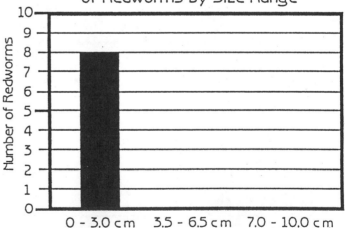

Questions

1. What is the average length of Nate's worms?_____

2. Which size range in the histogram had the most worms?_____

3. Which size range in the histogram had the fewest worms?_____

4. Tangi had the most worms in which size range?_____

WORMS EAT OUR GARBAGE Copyright © 1993 Flower Press

Graphing

Name _____ # Organizing Cocoons

Once someone goes to the effort of measuring large numbers of objects, how do they talk about what they found? How can they present their findings so that others will know what they discovered? One way is to make a graph of the numbers in an easy-to-read form. One such chart is a histogram, or bar graph. It is a series of blocks of different heights to compare different sets of measurements.

Wormformation

Directions

Mary, Joshua, and Erik each measured the lengths of seven cocoons with a metric ruler. The results are below. Place a mark in the correct size range on the Tally Chart for each length. Make a histogram. Answer the questions the follow. (*Hint: The first size range is done for you.*)

Mary

Cocoon	Length
1.	2.0 mm
2.	4.0 mm
3.	4.5 mm
4.	3.5 mm
5.	1.75 mm
6.	5.0 mm
7.	3.0 mm

Joshua

Cocoon	Length
1.	4.5 mm
2.	2.0 mm
3.	5.5 mm
4.	3.0 mm
5.	2.0 mm
6.	2.5 mm
7.	4.0 mm

Erik

Cocoon	Length
1.	5.0 mm
2.	3.5 mm
3.	2.0 mm
4.	2.5 mm
5.	4.0 mm
6.	3.0 mm
7.	1.75 mm

Tally Chart

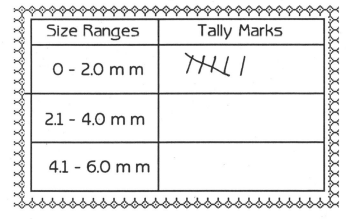

Size Ranges	Tally Marks
0 - 2.0 m m	ⅧⅠ
2.1 - 4.0 m m	
4.1 - 6.0 m m	

Total Numbers and Lengths of Cocoons by Size Range

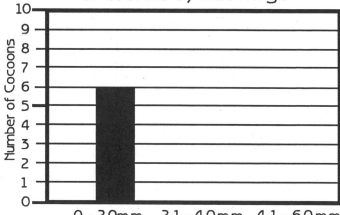

Questions

1. What is the average length of Mary's cocoons? _____
2. Which size range had the most cocoons? _____
3. Which size range had the fewest cocoons? _____
4. Joshua had the most cocoons in which size range? _____

Wormformation

Getting acquainted with something new takes time. Getting acquainted with a worm will not be the same as meeting a new friend because the worm will not be able to talk. You will have to ask questions of the worm, then think of how you can get the worm to answer your questions.

Materials

- moist paper towel
- ruler with metric and inch scales
- toothpicks
- shallow dish of water
- small tray
- 1 live worm

Directions

Slightly moisten a paper towel. Get a worm from its container and rinse it off in the dish of water. Place a toothpick under your worm in the water and transfer it to the moist paper towel. Watch it move. Use the toothpick as a tool to gently move and guide the worm. Answer the questions below. *Note: Remember to return the worm to its home to avoid stressing the animal.*

1. Does the worm try to get away? Describe its movement._____

_____

2. Does the worm try to avoid the toothpick when you place it in front of the worm?_____ Near the worm's tail?_____ Alongside the worm?_____

3. Do you see the swollen band, called a *clitellum*, on the worm? _____

4. Is the clitellum closer to the head end (*anterior*) or tail end (*posterior*) of the worm?_____

5. Which end of the worm is more pointed? anterior _____ posterior_____

6. Do you notice any difference in color from anterior to posterior?_____
Describe its color._____

_____

7. Does there appear to be a top side (*dorsal* side) or bottom side (*ventral* side)?_____
Use the adjectives *dorsal* and *ventral* to describe the differences you see._____

_____

_____

8. When you use your hand to make a shadow over the worm, does the worm seem to be less or more active? _____ Explain why._____

_____

Bonus Activity   Tell others about your new worm friend. Use the new words on this page to describe its anatomy and behavior.

Wormformation
Worms living in a worm bin normally eat wherever there is air, moisture, and food they like. You can train them, however, to eat food placed on the surface of the bedding. A light sprinkling of oatmeal placed on top of the bedding one day may be gone two days later. This is evidence that worms came to the surface to feed.

Materials
- 70 redworms
- oatmeal or oatbran
- measuring spoon
- 3 plastic containers with lids, such as 24 oz cottage cheese tubs
- vermicompost or garden soil

Directions
Follow the steps below to see how fast or slow the worms eat. Use the Observation Chart, page 161, to record observations and procedures. Answer the questions A - D at the end of the experiment.

1. Label containers as follows: 40 worms   20 worms   10 worms

2. For bedding, place vermicompost from your worm bin or moist garden soil in each container. Add the correct number of worms to each container.
3. Place oatmeal on top of bedding and moisten oatmeal with sprinkles of water.
4. Place lids with aeration holes on each container.
5. Set the containers in a dark place, such as a closet or cupboard.
6. Each day, take them out of the dark and observe the amount of oatmeal on top of the bedding in each container. Then, each day, add one new teaspoon of oatmeal to every container.
7. Record your observations daily. Write your conclusions after one week.

Questions to answer at the end of one week.

A. What happened to the oatmeal?_____

_____

_____

B. How much did the worms eat? In teaspoons (t)? _____ In tablespoons (T)?_____
   (Hint: Measure total amount of oatmeal eaten per container. 3 t = 1 T)

_____

_____

C. Did mold grow on the oatmeal? _____ In which containers?_____
   Describe the mold._____

D. Did the oatmeal disappear at the same rate in each of your 3 containers?
   Describe your results._____

_____

_____

Nature recycles mineral nutrients time and again. Many different kinds of organisms help to break down food waste into its nutrient minerals. These simple substances can be used as building blocks to make new plants and animals. This process of breaking down organic material into simpler substances is called *decomposition*. Microorganisms such as bacteria (too small to be seen without a microscope), molds (as seen on bread), and other fungi (such as mushrooms) are common decomposers.

Wormformation

Purpose
In this activity you will observe the growth of mold in different environments.

Materials
- muffin pan
- water
- vermicompost from worm bin
- measuring spoon
- vinegar
- slices of fruit or vegetable, such as
- paring knife
- sugar
  - apple, cucumber, or crookneck squash

Directions
1. Prepare a muffin pan with the following solutions and materials.
2. Slice the food into six pieces of equal size.
3. Place one slice into each cup of the muffin pan.
4. Set the muffin pan aside where you will not knock it over, and observe it for two weeks.
5. Record your observations once a week on the Decomposition Record Sheet, page 165.
6. At the end of 2 weeks, answer the three questions below.

Key
T = Tablespoon
t = teaspoon

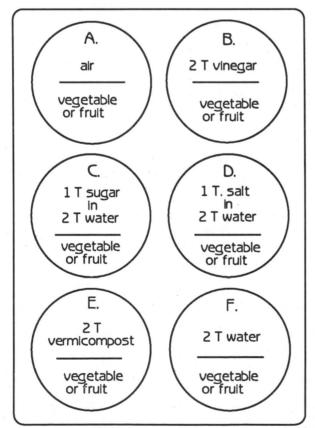

A.
air
___
vegetable or fruit

B.
2 T vinegar
___
vegetable or fruit

C.
1 T sugar in 2 T water
___
vegetable or fruit

D.
1 T. salt in 2 T water
___
vegetable or fruit

E.
2 T vermicompost
___
vegetable or fruit

F.
2 T water
___
vegetable or fruit

Questions
- Describe the mold in the food cup(s). (*Hint: What is the color, texture, shape, and size of the mold?*)
- Describe which foods did not decompose.
- Compare and describe the changes you saw in all the food cups.

Bonus Activity List some foods that are preserved by salt, vinegar, or sugar.

Name_____ **Observing the Bin**

Wormformation

As the worms adjust to their new home in the worm bin, changes will take place. They will make tunnels in the bedding. When you lift the lid you will see them quickly retreat down into the bedding to move away from the light.

Worms will digest the food they eat. Undigested matter such as soil will pass through their long intestine. The tiny, dark-colored masses the worms deposit are called worm castings. Other names for worm castings are worm manure or worm feces. Castings contain thousands of bacteria, humus, and many nutrients which help plants grow.

Directions

Observe changes in your worm bin. Write your observations in the spaces provided.

1. Find a worm casting. Where did you find it? Describe the worm casting.

   _____

   _____

2. Dig in the oldest garbage burying spot. What do you see? _____

   _____

   _____

3. Dig in the most recent burying spot. What do you see? _____

   _____

   _____

4. Compare your observations in #2 and #3. How are they alike and how are they different?

   _____

   _____

Bonus Activity Repeat the above observations in three weeks and compare the differences.

> The temperature in a worm bin may not be the same as the temperature in the room where the bin is located. Often, when decomposition is taking place, heat is given off. Some kinds of bacteria produce this heat as they multiply and decompose the organic waste. An instrument for measuring heat is the thermometer.
>
> **Wormformation**

Directions

To measure the decomposition heat in your worm bin, use a thermometer and record the temperature in nine different locations. Be sure to measure the room temperature so that you have a basis for comparison.

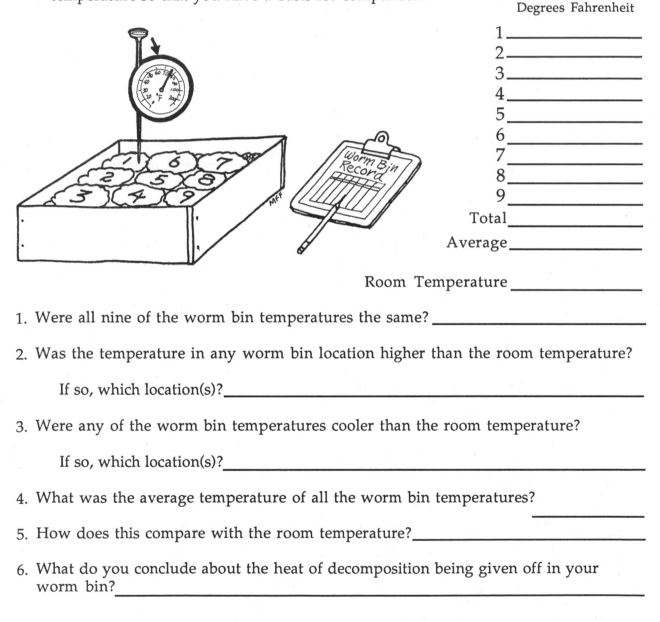

Degrees Fahrenheit

1 _____
2 _____
3 _____
4 _____
5 _____
6 _____
7 _____
8 _____
9 _____
Total _____
Average _____

Room Temperature _____

1. Were all nine of the worm bin temperatures the same? _____

2. Was the temperature in any worm bin location higher than the room temperature?

    If so, which location(s)?_____

3. Were any of the worm bin temperatures cooler than the room temperature?

    If so, which location(s)?_____

4. What was the average temperature of all the worm bin temperatures?
    _____

5. How does this compare with the room temperature?_____

6. What do you conclude about the heat of decomposition being given off in your worm bin?_____

_____

WORMS EAT OUR GARBAGE Copyright © 1993 Flower Press

Measurement

Name_____

Worm Bin Set Up	Garbage Record	Burying Locations

Worm Bin Set Up
Worm Bin Size _1'x2'x3'_
Lb of Worms _2_
Lb of Bedding _10_
Lb of Water _30_
Lb of Food _1_

Garbage Record
September 29
Set Up Date

Burying Locations

1	2	3
6	5	4
7	8	9

Date	Ounces of Garbage	Temp	Burying Location	Comments
9/29	32 oz	68°F	#1	Setup worm bin. Added bedding and garbage
9/30	0	78°F	—	Worms arrived today! Added to bin.
10/1	24 oz	80°F	#2	Added cucumbers, tomatoes, potatoes.
10/6	24 oz	79°F	#3	Added grapefruit rinds, banana peels.
10/13	16 oz	81°F	#4	Garbage disappearing in #1 and #2.
10/20	20 oz	79°F	#5	Garbage gone in #1. Added 2½ lb water.
10/25	24 oz	79°F	#6	Worms love bananas.
10/30	16 oz	80°F	#7	Lots of worms! Added ½ lb water.
11/6	22 oz	80°F	#8	Added dry newspaper shreds, 1½ lb.
11/13	24 oz	79°F	#9	Worms work in fresh bedding.

Directions

Use the Garbage Record to answer these questions. Round off numbers to the nearest whole number.

1. Calculate the following:

   A. total calendar days_____   D. total weeks_____

   B. total oz_____   E. average oz per day_____

   C. total lb_____   F. average lb per week_____

2. What was the temperature range?_____ What was the average temperature?_____

3. Why do you think the temperature increased during the observation period?
   _____

4. What did you learn from the comments?_____
   _____
   _____

> ## Wormformation
>
> It is easy to bury food waste in a worm bin. Select a spot, dig a hole with a garden fork in the bedding, and dump the scraps into the hole. Cover the scraps with bedding, close the lid, and that is it.
>
> Keeping track of how much food waste you bury helps you to learn more about the system. How can you tell your friends your worms ate 54 pounds of garbage in 4 months if you do not keep track?

Part I

Directions

Use the Garbage Record, page 81, as a reference and summarize results in words.

1. Write a paragraph summarizing data you analyzed from the Garbage Record.

   _____
   _____
   _____
   _____

2. Name two predictions based on the data from the Garbage Record.

   _____
   _____
   _____
   _____

Part II

Directions

Use the materials from the list below to complete activities A through F. Record the correct information in your Worm Bin Record, page 162.

Materials

- weight scale
- thermometer
- food waste
- food waste container
- garden fork
- Worm Bin Record

A. Weigh the food waste to be buried in the worm bin.
   (Hint: Remember to subtract the weight of the container from your final weight!)

B. Find the last burial spot recorded in the Worm Bin Record. Select the next spot.

C. Bury the garbage.

D. Insert a thermometer into the worm bin. Wait one minute, read the temperature, and record it on the Worm Bin Record. Measure and record the room temperature for comparison.

E. Record the date, weight of garbage in ounces, burial location, and your comments.

F. Complete the Part I exercises above using your own data.

When temperature, moisture, and food are favorable, a mature redworm can mate and produce two to three cocoons per week. Two to five* baby worms can hatch from each cocoon produced by a two-month old redworm. If one adult worm had 5 offspring a week for 26 weeks, it would produce 130 baby worms in six months (1 cocoon x 26 weeks x 5 hatchlings = 130). In eight weeks, the offspring can produce cocoons. In another eight weeks, their offspring can produce offspring. With each successive generation, young worms must compete with their parents for food.

All of the worms produce waste (castings). Bedding disappears as it is eaten and converted to castings. Conditions get crowded, and not all of the adult and baby worms live. The dead worms decompose rapidly in this active composting environment, so one rarely sees dead worms.

...AND THIS IS MY FAMILY!

Wormformation

Directions

Listed below are several things you can do to affect the worm population in a worm bin. If an action will increase the population, place an "up" arrow () in the <u>Increase</u> column. If the action will cause the worm population to decrease, place a "down" arrow (↓) in the <u>Decrease</u> column.

Increase   Decrease

Increase	Decrease	
☐	☐	Feed the growing population more food.
☐	☐	Remove vermicompost containing worms.
☐	☐	Put a predator, such as a mouse or a frog, into the worm bin.
☐	☐	Add fresh bedding.
☐	☐	Put the worms in a smaller bin.
☐	☐	Place worm bin in hot sun.
☐	☐	Take away the food supply of the worms.
☐	☐	Build a bigger worm bin.
☐	☐	Let the worm bin dry out.
☐	☐	Remove some of the worms and go fishing.
☐	☐	Let the worm bin freeze.

*Theoretical data provided by Michael Bisesi.

Wormformation Cocoons provide food and shelter for baby worms as they develop. It takes about three weeks before a baby redworm can hatch. A cocoon which is ready to hatch appears pinkish because of the red blood inside the baby worm. If you look at this cocoon carefully under a magnifying glass, you may be able to see the pulsing of a blood vessel in the baby worm. The tiny, transparent worm leaves its cocoon through a small fringed opening.

Materials

- 2 lids, one large, one small
- eyedropper and water
- tweezers
- magnifying glass
- ruler
- worm cocoons
- 2 flakes of oatmeal
- paper towel disks

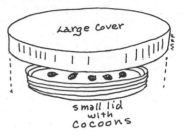

Large cover

small lid with cocoons

Directions

1. Find cocoons in your worm bin. Gently pick up 3 to 5 of them in your hand.

2. Place cocoons in the small lid that has a moistened disk of paper towel lining the bottom. Place 2 flakes of oatmeal with the cocoons as hatchling food.

3. Cover the cocoons with a second moistened disk. Keep the moisture in by covering the small lid with the large one. The large lid will keep light away from the cocoons.

4. Each day, for 5 days, observe your cocoons with a magnifying glass. Keep paper towel moist with a few drops of water if needed. *(Hint: Start this activity on Monday and end on Friday. Babies could dry out if left unattended during the weekend.)*

5. Count the cocoons and record the number on the Tally Chart. When a worm hatches record with one mark for each baby worm. Total the number of marks on Friday.

6. After your final count on Friday, measure the length of each baby worm. Then place babies and cocoons *and the moist paper disks* in the worm bin.

7. Write your observations and conclusions on the Observation Chart, page 161. Answer the questions below.

The length of each baby worm is: _____
_____

Daily Tally Chart	
Cocoons	
Baby Worms	

Questions

A. Did all of the baby worms hatch in the same day? _____
Explain why. _____

_____

B. Describe the color and average length of your hatchlings._____

_____

C. Describe the color of the cocoons before and after the worms have hatched.

_____

Worm Bin Animals

After the worm bin has been going for several months, animals other then earthworms often appear. These may include mites, ants, beetles, centipedes, snails, and other members of the compost community. If you added compost to your worm bin, you will probably find more kinds of organisms than if you used only newpaper for bedding.

Wormformation

Materials
- small container
- vermicompost from a worm bin
- small tray, such as a plastic meat tray
- toothpick

Directions
Borrow about a half cup of vermicompost from your worm bin. Place it on your tray. Use a toothpick as a tool to look for animals similar to those pictured below. Circle the ones you find. When your finish, return these animals and other organisms to the worm bin.

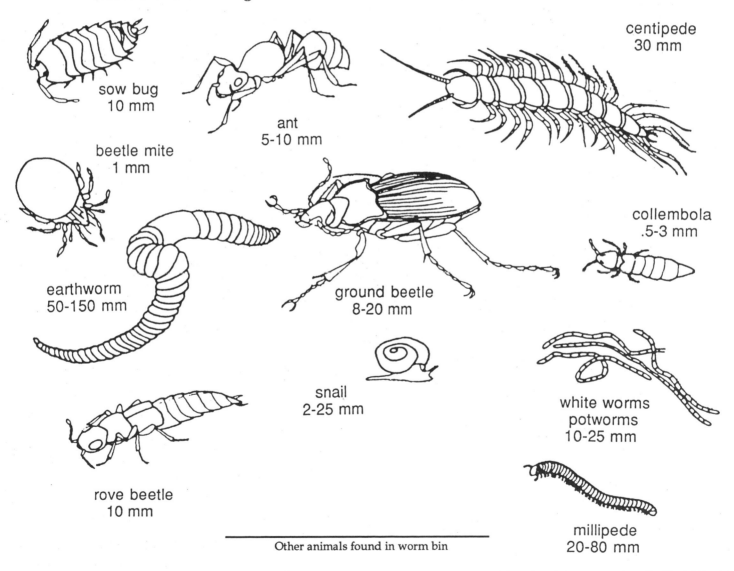

sow bug
10 mm

ant
5-10 mm

centipede
30 mm

beetle mite
1 mm

collembola
.5-3 mm

earthworm
50-150 mm

ground beetle
8-20 mm

snail
2-25 mm

white worms
potworms
10-25 mm

rove beetle
10 mm

millipede
20-80 mm

Other animals found in worm bin

Animals are not drawn to scale.

Adapted with permission from Dr. Daniel Dindal.

WORMS EAT OUR GARBAGE Copyright © 1993 Flower Press

Observation

Directions
Based upon your observations of the animals you found in the worm bin, answer the following questions.

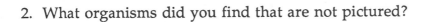

beetle mite
1 mm

centipede
30 mm

1. How many kinds of organisms did you find?

2. What organisms did you find that are not pictured?

collembola
.5-3 mm

3. What was the largest animal?

snail
2-25 mm

ant
5-10 mm

4. Which animal was fastest moving?

ground beetle
8-20 mm

5. Which animal seemed to have the most legs?

earthworm
50-150 mm

6. Did any animals roll up in a ball? _____ Which ones?

sow bug
10 mm

7. Why do you think an animal might roll up in a ball?

rove beetle
10 mm

8. Compare the size of the animals you saw. For example, the centipede was larger than the ant.

white worms
potworms
10-25 mm

The _____ was larger than the _____.

The _____ was larger than the _____.

millipede
20-80 mm

The _____ was larger than the _____.

The _____ was larger than the _____.

9. Which organisms did you find in the greatest number?

10. Compare your observations with two classmates. What did they find that you did not find?_____ What organism did you find that they did not find? _____

Bonus Activity   Number each 1/2 cup of vermicompost you and your friends examined. *(Hint: Call them Sample I, Sample II, and Sample III.)* Discuss why it is important to take more than one sample if you want to describe all of the organisms in a worm bin. Write your reasons.

Name _____

A worm bin contains many creatures other than earthworms. These creatures break down organic materials into simpler forms that can be reassembled into other kinds of living tissue. These decomposer organisms are true recyclers. To study them, you need to know something about what they look like, how big they are, and who eats whom.

Wormformation

Directions

This is a guessing game to help you identify animals which can sometimes be found in a worm bin. 1. Read all the descriptions. 2. Write 3 or more questions about the animals on the Question Cards, page 169. 3. Cut out each label. 4. Ask a friend to pick out and pin one of the labels on your back. 5. Use your question cards to try to guess which one it is. *(Hint: If you ask, "Do I have more than 8 legs?" and the answer is YES, then you are <u>not</u> an insect because an insect has 6 legs.)*

cut

Pill Bug or Roly-Poly

I am an isopod, which means that I have 10 pairs of legs that look very similar to each other. The flattened plates on my body make me look like an armadillo. I am about 1/2 inch long. I roll up in a ball if I am disturbed. I eat vegetation and leaf litter.

Centipede

I am a fierce hunter! I am known as a predator because I prey on earthworms and eat them. I have a pair of poison claws to help keep my prey from getting away. I move quickly on my many legs. I have only 1 pair of legs on each of my many (15-173) segments. I am about 1 to 2 inches long.

Ant

I am an insect with 6 legs and 3 body sections, head, thorax, and abdomen. I am an important decomposer because I break materials down into smaller particles. I create tunnels, and assemble soil particles into clumps. People find me a nuisance in their homes, so it's best to keep me from setting up residence in a worm bin.

Sow Bug

I am an isopod. I have ten pairs of legs. I am related to crayfish and lobsters. I breathe with gills, so I must live in a damp, moist place. My 1/2 inch body is oval and flat, with a series of flattened plates like my close relative, the roly-poly. However, I can't roll up in a ball. I eat vegetation and leaf litter.

Mite

I'm tiny. It could take 25 of us to cover an inch long line. My body is so round and fat it's hard to see my 8 jointed legs. Thousands of us live in a worm bin. We are important decomposers. Some of us eat plant material, such as mold and soft tissues of leaves. Others eat manure of other organisms. Some of us can harm earthworms, but not all worm bins have us.

Millipede

I have so many legs you would have a hard time counting them. My name means "thousand legs," but I don't have <u>that</u> many. Each segment has 2 pairs of legs. I'm not fierce, but quite timid. I roll up in a ball to avoid danger. I am a vegetarian. I eat soft, moist, decaying plants. I'm thick-skinned, dark-red in color, and 1 to 3 inches long.

cut

WORMS EAT OUR GARBAGE Copyright © 1993 Flower Press

Comprehension

Directions 1. Cut out the cards below.
2. Have a friend pin one on your back.
3. Try to guess who you are.

cut

Springtail (Collembola)

I am a tiny, white insect less than 1/16 inch long. I have a pointed prong folded beneath my abdomen. By quickly extending this "spring," I jump high into the air. When thousands of us gather on well-decomposed worm bedding, it looks as if we are jumping all over the place. We feed on molds and decaying matter and are important producers of humus.

cut

Collembola (co·lem'·bow la)

I am a close relative of the springtail, but I don't have the springing tail. I am tiny, often white, and less than 1/16 of an inch long. With the springtails, we are members of a group of animals which are primitive insects. I live with thousands of my companions in worm bins where I eat molds and decaying matter.

cut

Carabid Beetle (ca·rab·id)

I am an insect with shiny black, tough wings and am about 1/2 inch long. I live beneath stones, boards and other moist places. At night, I rapidly pursue my prey, such as slugs, and snails, and soft insects such as caterpillars. I am a fierce predator.

Earthworm

I am a long, thin soft-bodied animal. My body is made up of little rings called segments. I have neither legs nor eyes, but when I sense light, I slither away from it. I eat bacteria, fungi, protozoa, and decaying organic matter.

cut

Fruit Fly

I am a small fly. I am sometimes a nuisance. I don't bite, I don't sting, and I don't make annoying buzzing sounds. I never harm earthworms. People consider me a pest because I sometimes invade worm bins. If it's warm and moist, and fruit and yeast are present, I lay eggs and they hatch. One way to help keep me from being a nuisance is to hide food waste deep in the worm bin bedding. Usually I am present and you don't know it.

White Worm

I am a skinny, white worm also known as a pot worm, or an enchytraeid (en kee tray' id). I am about an inch long, but I am so thin I look like a frayed piece of thread. I move like an earthworm. In fact, we're related. I don't have red blood like an earthworm has. I eat well-decomposed material. You might think of me as one who likes to "finish-off" the job of decomposition.

cut

Food Web of the Compost Pile

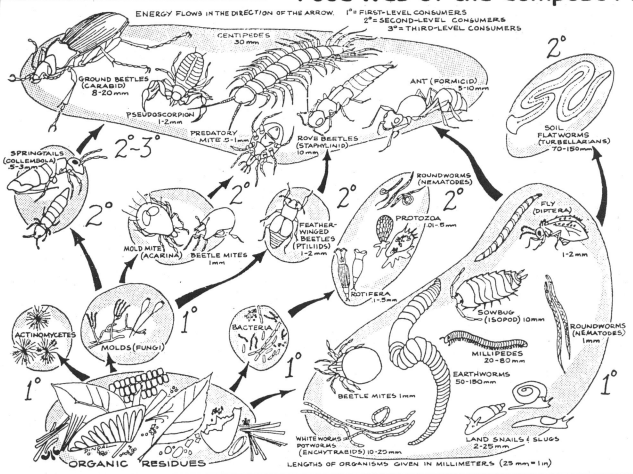

ENERGY FLOWS IN THE DIRECTION OF THE ARROW.   1°= FIRST-LEVEL CONSUMERS
2°= SECOND-LEVEL CONSUMERS
3°= THIRD-LEVEL CONSUMERS

CENTIPEDES 30 mm

GROUND BEETLES (CARABID) 8-20 mm

PSEUDOSCORPION 1-2 mm

ANT (FORMICID) 5-10 mm

2°

SOIL FLATWORMS (TURBELLARIANS) 70-150 mm

PREDATORY MITE .5-1 mm

ROVE BEETLES (STAPHYLINID) 10 mm

SPRINGTAILS (COLLEMBOLA) .5-3 mm

2°~3°

ROUNDWORMS (NEMATODES)

PROTOZOA .01-.5 mm

FLY (DIPTERA) 1-2 mm

2°

MOLD MITE (ACARINA)   BEETLE MITES 1 mm

FEATHER-WINGED BEETLES (PTILIIDS) 1-2 mm

2°

ROTIFERA .1-.5 mm

2°

ACTINOMYCETES

MOLDS (FUNGI)

1°

BACTERIA

1°

SOWBUG (ISOPOD) 10 mm

ROUNDWORMS (NEMATODES) 1 mm

MILLIPEDES 20-80 mm

EARTHWORMS 50-150 mm

1°

BEETLE MITES 1 mm

1°

WHITE WORMS POTWORMS (ENCHYTRAEIDS) 10-25 mm

LAND SNAILS & SLUGS 2-25 mm

ORGANIC RESIDUES

LENGTHS OF ORGANISMS GIVEN IN MILLIMETERS (25 mm = 1 in)

Many types of organisms in a worm bin break down organic materials to simpler forms
that can be recycled into other kinds of living tissue. A food web shows relationships
between organisms, based upon who eats whom. Dead organic materials are first
eaten by organisms like molds and bacteria. These are known as first-level (1°)
consumers. Earthworms, beetle mites, sowbugs, enchytraeids, and flies also consume
waste directly. First-level consumers are eaten by second-level (2°) consumers such
as springtails, mold mites, and protozoa. Third-level (3°) consumers are flesh-eaters,
or predators, which eat 1° and 2° consumers. Predators in a worm bin might include
centipedes, rove beetles, ants, and predatory mites.

Wormformation

Adapted with permission from Dr. Daniel Dindal

Directions

Answer the following questions, using the diagram and Wormformation to help you.

1. Give two examples of first-level consumers.

2. Give three examples of organisms which eat first-level consumers.

3. When an earthworm eats a dead leaf, what level consumer is it?

4. When an earthworm eats bacteria, what level consumer is it?

5. Give three examples of third-level consumers.

Bonus Activity   Humans are what level(s) consumer?

WORMS EAT OUR GARBAGE   Copyright © 1993 Flower Press

Diagram Interpretation

After a worm bin has been going for about 4 months, much of the bedding and garbage is converted to earthworm feces (manure), also called castings. As the proportion of castings increases, the quality of the environment for the worms decreases. They do not thrive eating their own manure. Other organisms, however, eat worm manure, breaking it down even further than the worms did. The manure from all the worm bin organisms becomes dark humus. It is called vermicompost because it is produced in a worm bin. People who use worm bins to produce vermicompost are called vermicomposters.

For the health of the worms, it is important to remove some of the vermicompost and replace it with new bedding after several months. An easy way to make room in a worm bin for new bedding and more garbage is to "divide and dump." Simply remove about two-thirds of the vermicompost in the worm bin and dump it directly on a garden or in a flower bed. Add fresh, properly moistened bedding to the vermicompost that is still in the bin. The remaining worms will multiply to provide enough worms for another garbage-eating cycle.

Wormformation

HARVESTING TECHNIQUE:
DIVIDE AND DUMP.

Materials
- bucket
- newspapers
- yard stick
- water
- scissors
- rubber gloves

1.
TAKE OUT ALL BUT
1/3 OF WORMS AND
VERMICOMPOST.
ADD NEW BEDDING.

2.
ADD VERMICOMPOST TAKEN
FROM BOX TO THE
GARDEN...WORMS
AND ALL.

Directions

Follow steps 1-6 to determine how much vermicompost to remove from your bin. Then follow the remaining steps to change the bedding.

1. Spread out the vermicompost in the worm bin so that the level is even.

2. Measure the length of the worm bin. The worm bin is _____ inches long.

3. Multiply the length by 1/3. For example, 1/3 x 24 inches = 8 inches.
    1/3 x_____ inches =_____ inches
         length

4. Measure the width of the worm bin. The worm bin is _____ inches wide.

5. Mark a large piece of paper (such as a newspaper) so that it is the width of the worm bin and 1/3 its length.

6. Cut the paper and lay it on top of the vermicompost to mark the 1/3 to be saved.

7. Remove 2/3 of the vermicompost (that which is not under the paper).

8. Prepare new bedding and add it to the side of the worm bin which is now empty.

9. Place vermicompost in a container, carry it to the garden, and deposit it there.

Directions

To find out how many worms are in a bin after several months, you will need to harvest them and change their bedding. Follow these steps. Before doing each step, predict what you think will happen. After completing the step, record your observations of what did happen.

Materials needed

- 6' x 6' sheet of heavy plastic
- container for worms
- heavy plastic bag for compost
- fresh bedding

Where are the worms?

How will it feel?

How will it smell?

Did the worm population increase?

Were my predictions correct?

What do I predict?

What will happen to the worms?

What will I see?

STEPS	PREDICTIONS	OBSERVATIONS
Spread the plastic on the ground or table. Dump the contents of the worm bin onto the plastic.		
Make about nine cone shaped piles. Shine the light on the piles. MAKE CONE-SHAPED PILES. BRIGHT LIGHT		
Scrape the vermicompost from the top of each pile. Place the compost in a container to use on garden and house plants.		
Place the worms in a container. Count the worms. Weigh the worms.		
Add the worms to bin with new bedding.		

> Most of us form opinions, or attitudes, about people we meet. We do this about animals as well. Some attitudes come from personal experience with animals. Others are formed by what we read or hear others say. Attitudes can be based on correct or incorrect information, fact or fiction. An opinion survey, or poll, can show wide ranges of beliefs or attitudes held in common. A poll makes it possible to count and report your findings.
>
> **Wormformation**

Directions (for surveyor)

To complete the survey, write two positive statements about worms on the lines 5 and 6. Ask a friend to respond to 1-6. Enter total of responses at the bottom of each column. Find the percent of total responses in columns Totally Agree, Maybe, and Never Agree. *(Hint: To find percent, divide the total possible per column by the total possible responses per column.)*

How Do I Feel About Worms?

_____ Attitude Statements _____

Directions (for friend)
How much do you agree or disagree with each statement? (check one)

	Totally Agree	Maybe	Never Agree
1. I would feel comfortable picking up and holding a worm.	☐	☐	☐
2. I think worms are fascinating.	☐	☐	☐
3. I would have a worm bin in my house, office, or school.	☐	☐	☐
4. I would save my table scraps to feed to worms.	☐	☐	☐
5. _____	☐	☐	☐
6. _____	☐	☐	☐

To be completed by surveyor

	Totally Agree	Maybe	Never Agree
Total responses per column	☐	☐	☐
Percent of all attitudes per column	☐	☐	☐

Bonus Activity Complete the survey yourself. Compare your answers with others.

Directions

At a neighorhood recyclers meeting, vermicomposters talk about their worms. Some of them have not got their facts right. Circle *true* or *false* below each statement. Draw <u>your</u> face as a cartoon and write a *true* worm statement in the empty "balloon" above your head.

1.
I have cocoons in my worm box that are as big as orange seeds.
true or false

2.
I didn't find any cocoons in my bin because my worms are immature.
true or false

3.
I leave a light on over my worm bin so the worms can see the food.
true or false

4.
The scientific name for my redworms is *Eisenia fetida*.
true or false

5.
I have 15 nightcrawlers to eat my family's food waste.
true or false

6.
I don't need to put fresh bedding in my worm bin for another 9 months.
true or false

Can You Prove It?

Wormformation

Fact: A thing that has actually happened, or is true; reality, truth, the state of things as they are. Example - A worm will continue to remain outside its burrow even if you shine a red light on it.

Opinion: A belief not based on certainty or positive knowledge, but on what seems true; what one thinks; a judgment. Example - Girls like having worms in the classroom.

Directions

In front of each statement, write "F" if it is fact and an "O" if it is opinion.

1. Worms like to wriggle when you hold them.

2. Earthworms eat tablescraps.

3. Worms are good pets.

4. Worms do not breathe like people do.

A worm in the hand is worth it.

5. Worms are important to other forms of life.

6. Worm castings can be used as plant fertilizer.

7. Every classroom should have a worm bin.

8. Earthworms do not have eyes.

9. Earthworms are "yucky."

10. Worms could take over the world.

Worms taking over the world.

Bonus Activity Write one fact and one opinion statement about worms.

Worms Go to School
(Headline)

Students Encouraged to Wriggle in Their Seats
(Subtitle)

Rita Perez
Gazette Reporter

F Thousands of pounds of worms are eating tons of garbage every year.
O They do so unnoticed and in the privacy of worm bins. And where are these worm bins? Inside peoples' homes! Your neighbor may have a worm bin and you do not know it. It is not that the neighbor is hiding anything from you. In fact, this process is so simple that the neighbor may forget to mention it. But the students in Pleasant Valley School are not hiding their worms from their neighbors. Each fall students in Ms. Fenwick's six grade class invite other classes and teachers to a worm party complete with "dirt cake" and "candy worms." Fenwick's students say they enjoy talking about slimy worms and yucky garbage to schoolmates. After

(Continued)

all, it is the "green" thing to do. When sixth grader Tisha Smith gave her "worm talk" at the party she asked everyone to wiggle like a worm. Says Smith, "If you think like a worm and act like a worm, you learn things about it." Donald Jenkinson dug around in the classroom worm bin and pulled up a red wriggler. "This," he said, "is our garbageman." This reporter asked: "What happened to visiting police and fire fighters in the classroom?" "We look forward to a visit from them, too," said Fenwick, " but it is exciting to see students thinking about garbage, live worms, and solutions to our waste problems." Unlike most teachers who try to keep students from wriggling in their seats, Fenwick says, "Just think what the kids would be doing if we studied frogs!" Well, if wriggling and jumping help kids learn better, I say it is a "can of worms" that needs to be opened. Hmm, I wonder if a worm bin in the Gazette press room would go over? _____

Directions
Read the news article. Pick out the reporter's lines of humor (H), quotes (Q), opinion (O), and fact (F). Place the correct letter code on or close to the line. Two are done for you. Then write your own news "wormy" lines below. *(Hint: Read Idea Starters.)*

Idea Starters
- I asked 25 people what they thought of worms . . .
- I asked my neighbors if they would use a worm bin . . .
- I observed worms . . .
- How to keep worms happy . . .

1. Write a humorous line for a news story.

   _____

   _____

2. Write a quote (which is something someone said).

   _____

   _____

3. Write an opinion of your own or someone else.

   _____

   _____

4. Write a fact you know to be true.

   _____

   _____

Bonus Activity Write a worm news article with a friend. Start with a headline and subtitle.

A party is for fun, but it can be educational, too. It is very important to make sure your guests will have a good time as well as learn something. Planning the party on paper helps you to be better prepared. It allows you to put ideas in the right order. A good plan includes tasks to be done, materials needed, dates of events, locations, and names of persons to carry out each task.

Plan a party to welcome your worms. Invite another class or group of friends to meet your worms and learn about your worm bin.

Wormformation

Directions

Read the Wormformation. Jot down items on the lines below as you think of them. Next, copy items to the Project Planning Sheet, page 160, by placing them in the order to be carried out. Give the correct date, place, and person beside each item. *(Hint: Here are a few ideas to get you started.)*

Party location will be at . . .

Number of guests will be . . .

We will invite . . .

Games to play . . .

Refreshments will be . . .

Everyone must bring or tell about . . .

Things to buy or make are . . .

Give "worm talks" to guests on . . .

Party Ideas

_____
_____
_____
_____
_____
_____
_____
_____
_____
_____
_____
_____

Materials needed
- paper
- markers, paints, or crayons
- ruler
- scissors

Directions
Follow the steps to make an invitation to send to worm party guests.

Step 1. Fill in the information needed in section D.
Step 2. Color Section B.
Step 3. Cut out the invitation.
Step 4. Fold paper in half so that Section A is on the left with the fold on the top.
Step 5. Fold in half again so that Section B is the front of the invitation.

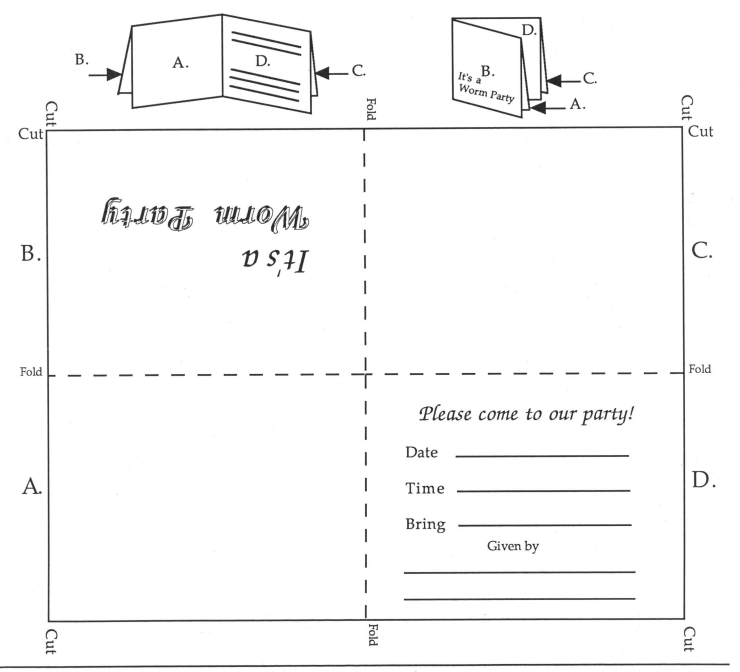

It's a
Worm Party

Please come to our party!

Date _____

Time _____

Bring _____

Given by

_____

_____

Worm Party Games

What is a party without games? Planning games for a worm party can be a lot of fun because you can use your imagination. Think of favorite games you like to play. Ask yourself how the worms fit into the game. Think up new rules to fit your "wormy" game.

Wormformation

Ideas for Wormy Games

Game 1: "Worm says . . ."   Play this variation of "Simon says . . ." Have the leader randomly ask the students to take action. For example, "Worm says . . .wiggle like a worm."   "Worm says . . . don't step on a worm."

Directions

Write more commands for "Worm says . . . " in the box below. Play this game with a friend.

"Worm says . . ."

_____   _____

_____   _____

_____   _____

_____

Game 2: "Worm Bee" Play this variation of a spelling bee. Before the bee, prepare a spelling list of words related to worms.

Directions

Use references to spell words for the Worm Bee. Pick simple words as well as hard ones.

Spelling List

_____

_____

_____

_____

_____

_____

_____

_____

_____

Game 3: Think of a favorite game. Write the rules below to make it a "wormy" game.

_____
Name of Game

Rules:

_____

_____

_____

_____

_____

_____

_____

Name_____   # The Dirt Cake Recipe

Materials needed

- - - - - - - • 1   3 qt plastic flower pot - - - - - -
- - - - - - - • 3   large mixing bowls - - - - - -
- - - - - - - • 2   measuring cups   - - - - - -
- - - - - - - • 3   stirring spoons   - - - - - -
- - - - - - - • 3   artificial flowers   - - - - - -

Directions

Double and triple the Dirt Cake recipe on the dotted lines below.
(Hint: The first ingredient has been done for you.) Use this recipe
to make a special "dirt" cake for your friends. Follow steps 1 -7 below.

Double the
Recipe
Here
2 lb

Triple the
Recipe
Here
3 lb

Dirt Cake

Ingredients:
    1   1 lb package chocolate, cream-filled cookies
    2   8-ounce packages cream cheese
    1/4 cup margerine or butter
    1   cup powdered sugar
    1   5.9 oz packages of instant chocolate pudding
    3   cups milk
    1   8 oz non-dairy whipped topping
    1   package candy worms
                 - Yields about 24 one-half cup servings

1. Crush cookies into bowl #1.

2. Mix together cream cheese, butter, and powdered sugar in bowl #2.
   (Hint: allow ingredients to warm up to room temperature.)

3. Make chocolate pudding with milk in bowl #3.
   (Hint: Follow directions on package.)

4. Fold whipped cream into pudding in bowl #3.

5. Mix ingredients in bowl #3 with bowl #2. Blend well.

6. In a clean, plastic flower pot, layer the creamed ingredients with
   the crushed cookies. Start with crushed cookies in the bottom of
   the pot. End with crushed cookies as the top layer.

7. Decorate your cake with candy worms and artificial flowers.
   Eat immediately or refrigerate.

_____

Other ideas: Use individual small flower pots instead of one big one. Try making
the recipe with other kinds of cookies or cake mixes. Try different puddings.

Bonus Activity   Calculate how many additional flower pots, bowls, and flowers
                    you will need to double and triple the recipe. Write your answers
                    beside the **Materials Needed** list. Explain your answers to a friend.

Directions

Make up badges to pin on and wear. Trade them with your friends or give them to guests. Draw and color each badge. Write a short phrase or sentence on each badge that gives information about worms. It can be a serious thought or a funny one. Cut out and wear them at a Worm Party or other event. *(Hint: The first one is done for you.)*

Write phrases or sentences here before making a badge._____

_____

_____

_____

_____

_____

Directions

You will need to keep your worms safe and healthy when you are not there to maintain your worm bin. Make a list of rules for "worm-sitters" to follow when you are away. *(Hint: Use memos and reminders found on the outer edges of page as key ideas.)*

Rules for Worm-Sitters

Thank you for being willing to take care of the worms while I am away. Follow these simple rules:

_____
_____
_____
_____
_____
_____
_____
_____
_____
_____
_____
_____

Notes
Give us fresh bedding

LOOK!
Don't overfeed us!

Reminder:
Remove dense castings

MEMO
Don't let us dry out

Feed us

We like moisture

"Read the one about humans make good friends."

We like the dark

Talk to us

Don't turn the heat off

Worm Bin-Time Stories

We like to be covered

Worm Bin Riddles

Directions
Now that you are acquainted with
your worm bin, answer the riddles.

1. I am shredded, lumpy, damp, and gray.

   _____

2. I have more than 6 legs and roll into a ball
   when stressed.

   _____

3. I eat bacteria.

   _____

4. I rot and provide food for bacteria in the
   worm bin.

   _____

5. I am a pest to humans, but the worms do not
   mind having me around.

   _____

6. I can be square and wooden, square and plastic,
   round and plastic, or round and metal.

   _____

7. I am like an earthworm, but look like a white
   piece of thread.

   _____

8. I look like a tiny lemon and babies hatch from me. _____

WORMS EAT OUR GARBAGE Copyright © 1993 Flower Press

Reasoning

There are more than 70,000 types of soil in North America. One way to classify soil is by texture (feel).
- Clayey soils are smooth, sticky, and dense. They hold water so tightly it is less available to plants.
- Sandy soils are very gritty, loose, and crumbly. They hold little water for plants.
- Loamy soils are a mixture of the above soils. They are loose, crumbly, and hold water well for use with plants.

Soils can also be classified by color.
- dark - black, dark grey, or dark brown
- medium - brown to yellow brown
- light - pale brown to yellow

Wormformation

The darker the color, the more organic material is in the soil. In general, the darker the soil, the more easily water sinks in, and the better it is for growing plants.

Directions

1. Dig up a sample of soil, such as soil from a garden, barren field, woods, or empty lot. Put the sample in a container.

2. Examine your soil. Wet a small sample and rub it between your fingers.

3. Use the Wormformation to complete the data card below. Attach it to your sample.

O   Soil Sample Data Card

Where found _____
                              location

Description   color _____

                 smell _____

                 texture (feel) _____

                 other _____

Soil type _____

Prediction for growing plants ☐ Good ☐ Fair ☐ Poor

Reason for prediction_____

_____

Bonus Activity   Share your soil samples with a friend. In what ways are they alike? In what ways are they different?

Observation

Worm Growth in Soils

Melissa Howe's Science Fair Project - A Story

> Scientists call an educated guess about the outcome of an experiment a hypothesis. They use their hypothesis to guide their thinking about how to collect observations or to conduct an experiment. Part of the process of scientific discovery is to test a hypothesis. To test a hypothesis, a scientist asks questions to find out whether the hypothesis is true (accepted) or not true (rejected).
>
> **Wormformation**

Melissa wanted to know which soils help multiply worms and which soils support worm growth in order to aerate the soil and make it more fertile for growing crops. There were nine different soil types on her family's Michigan farm. Melissa believed that different soil types would affect the growth of worms. She used this topic for her science fair project.

Melissa made an educated guess that two of the soil types, Adrian muck and Houghton muck, would support the growth of worms better than most soils. She also predicted that clay soils would not sustain a healthy environment for worms. She had three hypotheses.

1. Soils differ in their ability to support the growth of worms.
2. Adrian and Houghton mucks will support the growth of worms better than other soils.
3. Clay soils will not sustain a healthy environment for worms.

Melissa had to identify a way to measure growth. The worm species Melissa selected was *Lumbricus rubellus*, a redworm species known to live in soils with high organic matter. She measured the change in worm length and worm weight over a four-week period.

Melissa also wanted to know which soil types help worms to multiply. To measure this, she decided to count the baby worms and cocoons present in the soil samples after four weeks. She chose four weeks to give adult worms time to lay cocoons and baby worms time to hatch from the cocoons. Melissa set up data sheets to record beginning and ending worm length, beginning and ending worm weight, and number of baby worms and cocoons.

Melissa set up the following experiment. She added a shallow layer of crushed limestone to the bottom of 10 one gallon jars. Melissa then labeled the jars and filled each with a sample of soil corresponding to the jar's label. The tenth jar contained moistened shredded newspaper. She didn't know whether the different soils would support the kind of worms she was using, but she knew they could live in newspaper bedding, so the tenth jar served as a control for her experiment.

Melissa measured and recorded the total worm length and the total worm weight for ten batches of 50 worms (*Lumbricus rubellus*). She placed each batch in a jar and wrapped the jars with black plastic to keep out the light. She maintained her cultures by adding food (a formula of ground grains) daily and removing moldy food when necessary.

After four weeks, Melissa carefully examined the contents of each jar. She counted, weighed, and measured the worms, recording her findings on her record sheets. She and her family (there was so much work to do, everyone was involved by now) were amazed to find that in some soils there were over 200 baby worms!

Used with permission from Melissa Howe.

Directions

Read the story about Melissa's research, **Worms: Growth in Soils**, page 104. Answer the questions below.

1. Use a dictionary and define these words.

   hypothesis

   prediction

   scientist

   accept

   reject

2. What does it mean to "test a hypothesis?"

3. What did Melissa want to find out?

4. How did Melissa measure worm growth in her research?

5. How did Melissa measure which soil types help worms to multiply?

6. Did this story contain information that would allow you to accept or reject her hypotheses?

   Explain.

Bonus Activity What one question do you have about worms? Make an educated guess about the answer to this question. Design a research project to test your hypothesis. Present this research proposal to your class.

Name_____   **Fox Sandy Loam**

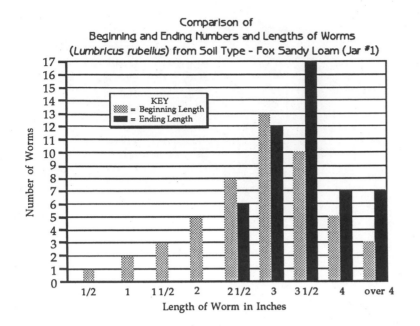

Comparison of
Beginning and Ending Numbers and Lengths of Worms
(*Lumbricus rubellus*) from Soil Type - Fox Sandy Loam (Jar #1)

KEY
= Beginning Length
= Ending Length

Number of Worms (y-axis)
Length of Worm in Inches (x-axis)

Soil Information

Fox Sandy Loam is made of sandy soil, clay, and organic matter. Water drains well from this soil type because it is formed on a sandy base. The organic matter should provide food and hold enough moisture to support worm growth.

Jar # 1
Fox Sandy Loam
Soil Type

Directions

Read the story of Melissa's **Worms: Growth in Soils**, page 104. Study the graph and chart which she presented in her report. Answer the questions below.

R E S U L T S

	Beginning	Ending
Total Length of Worms	144.5 inches	166.5 inches
Average Length Per Worm	2.89 inches	3.39 inches
Total Weight of Worms	12.6 grams	18.9 grams
Average Weight Per Worm	.25 grams	.385 grams
TOTAL: **ADULT POPULATION**	50	49
TOTAL: **BABIES**	0	125
TOTAL: **COCOONS**	0	5

Data used with permission from Melissa Howe

1. At the beginning of Melissa's experiment, how many worms were 3 inches long?_____

2. At the beginning of the experiment, how many worms were 1/2 inch long?_____

3. How long were the longest worms at the beginning?_____

4. What was the total length of worms at the end of the observation period?_____

5. What was the total increase in worm length during the 4 weeks?_____

6. What was the beginning weight of worms?_____

7. How much more did they weigh at the end of the 4 weeks?_____

Name _____

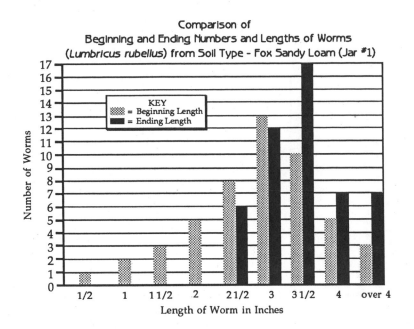

Comparison of
Beginning and Ending Numbers and Lengths of Worms
(*Lumbricus rubellus*) from Soil Type - Fox Sandy Loam (Jar #1)

KEY
= Beginning Length
= Ending Length

Number of Worms

Length of Worm in Inches

Soil Information

The lifting and blowing of soil by wind is known as wind erosion. Loss of topsoil occurs readily in sandy loam soils if they are not protected from blowing winds. One way to protect soil from wind erosion is to keep it covered with plants at all times. As plants add to the organic matter in the soil, they also provide food for worms.

Directions

Read the story **Worms: Growth in Soils**, page 104. Study the graph and chart which Melissa presented in her report. Answer the questions below.

RESULTS	Beginning	Ending
Total Length of Worms	144.5 inches	166.5 inches
Average Length Per Worm	2.89 inches	3.39 inches
Total Weight of Worms	12.6 grams	18.9 grams
Average Weight Per Worm	.25 grams	.385 grams
TOTAL: ADULT POPULATION	50	49
TOTAL: BABIES	0	125
TOTAL: COCOONS	0	5

Data used with permission from Melissa Howe

1. What was the average increase in weight for each worm?_____

2. Did all worms survive the 4 weeks?_____

3. Did the population of worms increase?_____

4. How many worms were in the final population?_____

5. At the end of the 4-week period, what was the most common worm length?_____

6. Generally speaking, at the end of 4 weeks, almost all the adult worms were between

_____ and _____ inches long.

Bonus Activity   Based on Melissa's observation, would you conclude that Fox Sandy Loam supported the growth of worms? Tell why.

A Soil Called Marl

Comparison of
Beginning and Ending Numbers and Lengths of Worms
(*Lumbricus rubellus*) from Soil Type - Marl (Jar #5)

KEY
▒ = Beginning Length
■ = Ending Length

Number of Worms

Length of Worm in Inches

R E S U L T S	Beginning	Ending
Total Length of Worms	144.5 inches	48 inches
Average Length Per Worm	2.89 inches	2.67 inches
Total Weight of Worms	12.4 grams	3.9 grams
Average Weight Per Worm	.25 grams	0.12 grams
TOTAL: ADULT POPULATION	50	18
TOTAL: BABIES	0	14
TOTAL: COCOONS	0	0

Data used with permission from Melissa Howe

Directions

Melissa presented this graph in her report. Answer the questions which follow.

1. How many worms were 2 1/2 inches long <u>or longer</u> at the beginning of Melissa's experiment?

2. How many worms were less than 2 inches long at the beginning?

3. Did the total worm length increase or decrease? _____ By how much?

4. How do you explain the fact that the average length per worm was very similar, yet total worm length was much less at the end of 4 weeks?

5. How many adult worms failed to survive the 4-week period?

6. Did Melissa find any cocoons after 4 weeks?

7. Would you conclude that the marl soil type supported the growth of earthworms? _____ Why?

Jar #5

Marl
Soil Type

Interpretation of Data

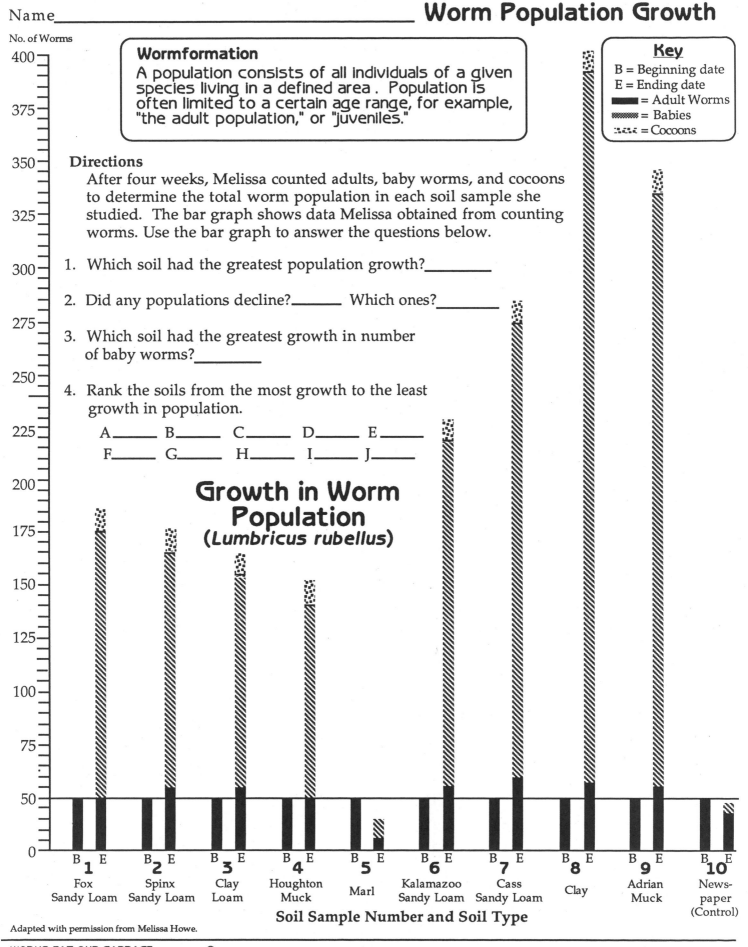

No. of Worms

Wormformation
A population consists of all individuals of a given species living in a defined area. Population is often limited to a certain age range, for example, "the adult population," or "juveniles."

Key
B = Beginning date
E = Ending date
█ = Adult Worms
▦ = Babies
≈ = Cocoons

Directions
After four weeks, Melissa counted adults, baby worms, and cocoons to determine the total worm population in each soil sample she studied. The bar graph shows data Melissa obtained from counting worms. Use the bar graph to answer the questions below.

1. Which soil had the greatest population growth?_____

2. Did any populations decline?_____ Which ones?_____

3. Which soil had the greatest growth in number of baby worms?_____

4. Rank the soils from the most growth to the least growth in population.

A____ B____ C____ D____ E____
F____ G____ H____ I____ J____

Growth in Worm Population
(*Lumbricus rubellus*)

Soil Sample Number and Soil Type

1 Fox Sandy Loam
2 Spinx Sandy Loam
3 Clay Loam
4 Houghton Muck
5 Marl
6 Kalamazoo Sandy Loam
7 Cass Sandy Loam
8 Clay
9 Adrian Muck
10 Newspaper (Control)

Adapted with permission from Melissa Howe.

A population of organisms can change by increasing or decreasing. Two ways that populations <u>increase</u> are through reproduction and immigration. Populations increase when adults produce offspring, and when other members of that species move into the area defined by the original population. A population explosion occurs when a population increases very rapidly because the conditions are very favorable for reproduction and survival of the offspring.

Populations <u>decrease</u> when individuals die or move out of the area. Sometimes an environmental disaster causes many individuals to die in a short time. This is called a population crash.

In some instances, adults produce many offspring because conditions are <u>not</u> favorable for survival of the offspring. Many offspring are produced on the chance that at least two will survive to replace the adults and maintain the population.

Wormformation

Directions

Calculate the percentage of change in population for each soil type. These are the steps to follow:

1. Subtract beginning worm count from final worm count. This gives you the change in the number of worms. Write that number in the D column in the chart below.

2. Divide change in number of worms by the beginning number of worms (which will always be 50 in this experiment). Write that number in the E column. This gives you a factor for the change in worm population. Use a plus sign (+) for an increase in population. Use a minus sign (-) for a decrease in population.

3. Multiply the factor for the change in worm population by 100. Write that number in the F column. This gives you the percent of change in the worm population over the 4-week period of Melissa's experiment.

4. Use the histograms of **Worm Population Growth**, page 109, to complete the rest of the chart for Clay soil and Adrian muck.

Change in Worm Populations Over a Four-Week Period

A Soil type	B Beginning number of worms	C Ending number of worms	D Change in number of of worms	E Factor for population change	F Percent change
Fox sandy loam	50	175	125	2.5	+250%
Houghton muck	50	140			
Marl	50	32			
Clay					
Adrian muck					

Data used with permission from Melissa Howe

5. Which soil type showed the greatest change in population? _____

Name_____   **Fact or Opinion**

Scientists use factual information to support their opinions. They collect data in an orderly manner. They make and record observations. They measure. They use numbers. They use tools and instruments. A tool can be as simple as a ruler or a scale. An instrument might be an electronic balance or a microscope.

Scientists then review and analyze the data they collect. From the analysis they develop an opinion about what this means. Opinions can be based upon fact or upon feelings. It is important for everyone to be able to tell which opinions are supported by factual information.

Wormformation

Directions

Read the following notes from Melissa's science report, looking for examples of statements which are either fact or opinion. Put a check in the chart to tell if each statement is fact or opinion.

"Newspapers were used as the control. In the end, looking through this was probably my favorite job of the whole experiment. The newspaper looked like Swiss cheese but smaller, and had a million times more holes. It was so neat to look at the results of the worms in this jar. Plus it was super easy to find worms. The papers smelled very moldy and we only found four babies and not one single cocoon. We looked through the papers which were sticky and slimy two times just to be sure. I wouldn't recommend trying to grow worms in this because the population did not really change. I believe this is because the newspapers do not have enough nutrients as the soil in order to populate the worms. However, the worms can eat it since it is made from plant fiber."

-Melissa Howe. *Worms: Growth in Soils*

<u>Statements</u>

Fact	Opinion

- newspapers were the control
- my favorite job
- newspaper looked like Swiss cheese
- had a million times more holes
- it was neat to look at
- the papers smelled moldy
- we found only four babies
- we looked through the papers two times
- we did not find a single worm
- I wouldn't recommend trying to grow worms
- the population did not change
- I believe the newspapers do not have enough nutrients
- [newspaper] is made from plant fiber

Used with permission from Melissa Howe.

Good soil is alive. It is the home of many kinds of plants and animals. Most (such as bacteria, fungi, and protozoa) are so small they cannot be seen without a microscope. The following animals are big enough to see:

1. worms (such as earthworms that have no legs)
2. grubs (wormlike animals with legs)
3. snails and slugs (soft-bodied animals; snails have shells, slugs do not)
4. insects (animals with 3 pairs of jointed legs)
5. spiders and mites (animals with 4 pairs of legs)
6. animals with more than 4 pairs of legs

Wormformation

Materials

- soil collected from a depth of 3 inches (about a cup per person)
- 6 small clear bottles and lids with holes (one for each category listed in Wormformation)
- magnifying glass
- microscope (if available)
- tweezers
- shallow tray or pie pan

Directions

1. Pour soil on the tray or pie pan.
2. Sort the soil and look for living things.
3. Put the animals into different bottles.
   (Like animals can be placed in the same bottle.)
4. Label the bottles according to the animals found.
5. Draw pictures of your animals in the correct categories below.
6. Return the live animals to outdoor soil.

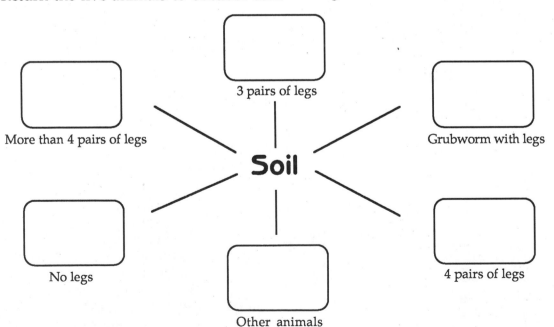

More than 4 pairs of legs

3 pairs of legs

Grubworm with legs

Soil

No legs

Other animals

4 pairs of legs

Bonus Activity Compare your soil findings with the soil sample taken by a friend.

Cheryl grows food organically. That is, she uses no synthetic fertilizers and pesticides. Instead, she creates favorable conditions for billions of soil organisms to assist her in nourishing the plants. She keeps weeds down by placing straw and shredded leaves on paths between the rows. This mulch also helps to retain water in the soil so that the plants do not dry out. Cheryl tries not to have bare ground in her garden for very long because heavy rains could wash the soil away.

Wormformation

If you were to pick up a teaspoonful of the rich soil in Cheryl's garden, it could contain as many as four billion bacteria. It also would have tangles of microscopic threads of fungi that could extend from 120 feet to 300 feet if stretched out in a line. "Fungi-like bacteria" called actinomycetes are also present by the million. These organisms resemble bacteria in some ways, and fungi in others. If the soil was damp, it would contain millions of protozoa living in the thin film of water around each soil particle.

Only with the aid of a powerful microscope could you see the billions of organisms living in that teaspoonful of soil. What most people do not know is that healthy soil is living soil.

The Living Soil Beneath My Feet

MULCH

~Bacteria
~Protozoa
~Actinomycetes
(ak·tin´·o·my·cee´·tees)

Directions
Use references and Wormformation to answer the questions.

1. What does it mean to grow food organically? _____
_____

2. What is mulch?_____
_____

3. What are two advantages of using mulch?_____
_____

4. What are bacteria?_____
_____

5. What are actinomycetes? _____
_____

6. What are fungi? _____
_____

7. What are protozoa? _____
_____

8. What is *living soil*? _____
_____

WORMS EAT OUR GARBAGE Copyright © 1993 Flower Press   Comprehension

How to Set Up a Soil Profile

Directions

Follow these steps to set up a soil profile. Write your description of each layer on the *Soil Profile Observation Chart*, page 172.

Materials

1. Soil profile/worm observation chamber or any container that is transparent, such as an aquarium, terrarium, or glass jar. (See *How to Build a Worm and Soil Profile Observation Chamber*, page 163 for instructions on how to construct this 3 gal chamber.)

2. Three gallons of soil horizon materials in the quantities given below:

   - leaves
   - 2 qt compost
   - 1 pt fine white sand
     (to use as a marker)
   - 3 qt topsoil
   - 4 qt subsoil
   - 1 qt small rocks,
     1-2 inches in diameter

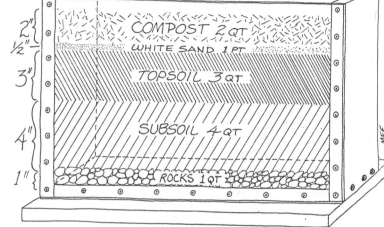

Procedure

Starting from the bottom, place about 1 qt of small rocks in the soil profile chamber. These represent the lowest layer, known as the C Horizon, or sometimes called the parent material. The C Horizon has little living matter. It may show some weathering, but less than the layers on top of it.

Next place about 4 qt of subsoil. Subsoil, the B Horizon, may be brown, red, yellow, or gray. It may be quite sandy. If made up of clay, it will be hard when dry, and stickier when wet than surrounding soil layers. This middle soil layer contains few organisms, but plant roots may penetrate into it.

Plac about 3 qt of topsoil on top of the subsoil. Known as the A horizon, healthy topsoil teems with life. Plant roots, bacteria, fungi, and small animals make topsoil a living system. Because it has more organic matter, topsoil is darker than subsoil.

Place the white sand on top of the topsoil. This is an <u>artificial layer</u> not found in a natural soil profile. It serves as a marker to help with your observations.

Add 2 qt of compost for the O, or Organic horizon. Compost is partially decomposed organic matter such as leaves, garden residue, and food waste. In its active state, compost contains millions of microorganisms and other soil-dwelling organisms which consume the ever-changing organic matter and each other. Finally, add a thin layer of leaves to the surface.

Thanks to Kim Davison, Lincoln School for International Studies, Kalamazoo, MI for inspiring this idea.

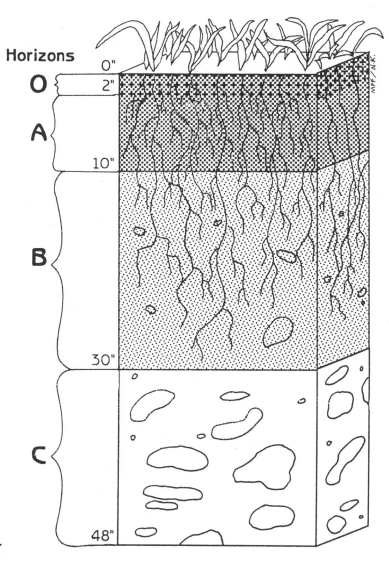

Horizons

O   0"
     2"
A
     10"

B

     30"
C

     48"

Wormformation

The profile of a soil is specific to a particular site. The thickness of each layer varies depending on location, use, erosion, and other factors. For example, a plowed field may not have organic matter lying on its surface. Although a flood plain may have a thick topsoil horizon, a desert will have none.

This soil profile is an example of one which might be present in a pasture in mid-western North America.

Directions
Read Wormformation and use the diagram to answer the questions below.

1. How thick is each horizon? O_____ A_____ B_____ C_____

2. How many inches is the top of the A horizon below the surface? _____

3. How many inches is the bottom of the A horizon below the surface?_____

4. How many inches is the top of the B horizon below the surface? _____

5. How many inches is the bottom of the B horizon below the surface?_____

6. How many inches below the surface is the top of the C horizon? _____

7. How many inches below the surface is the bottom of the C horizon?_____

Bonus Activity Describe the materials and plants you see in each horizon. In what ways are they alike? In what ways are they different?

Scientists need to be good observers in order to document their findings and report to others. Scientists communicate their findings in pictures and words.

Wormformation

Directions

Draw layers of the Soil Profile in correct order. Label each layer.

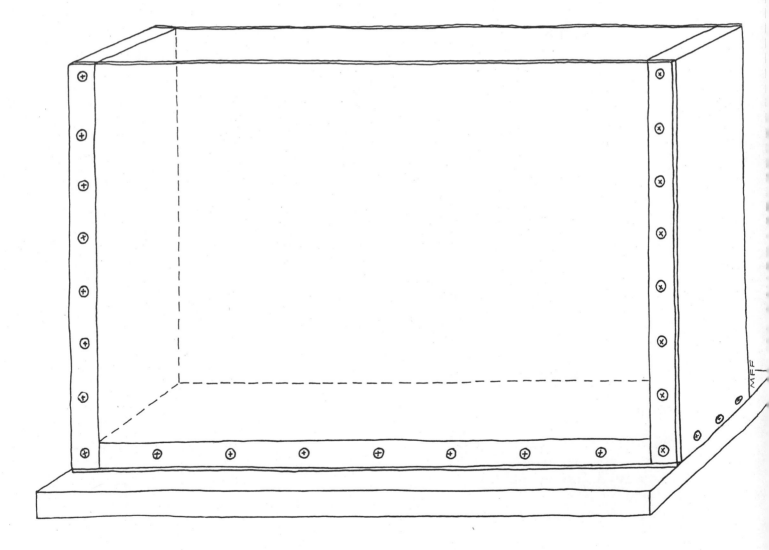

Thanks to Kim Davison, Lincoln School for International Studies, Kalamazoo, MI for inspiring this idea.

Recording

How to Set Up and Maintain a Worm Observation Chamber

_____

Name

Materials and worm types
- a loose top for your chamber to allow for air and to prevent moisture from evaporating too quickly
- a dark cover of loosely woven material or cardboard to cover the chamber when not being observed.
- worms, preferably at least two different kinds; good choices might be up to 20 redworms, 2 dew worms (nightcrawlers), and 3 garden worms

Directions

Follow these steps to convert your soil profile chamber to a worm observation chamber.

1. Put worms on top of the organic matter in your chamber. Observe their reactions to this new environment.

2. Add a tablespoon or so of food for the worms to the top layer. Examples of food are leaves, vegetables, and oatmeal or corn meal. _Hint: Different kinds of worms eat different foods, so a variety of foods is better._

3. Check your worm observation chamber weekly. Add water and food as needed.

4. Observe the changes in the chamber. Record your observations on the chart, _Log of Worm Observation Chamber_, page 118, using words and pictures.

Additional hints:
- Remove moldy food.

- Remember, the more worms you have, the more maintenance will be required. More worms means more food and more housekeeping.

- Properly maintained, this observation chamber should serve as a good environment for the worms for a school year. Return the worms to a moist place outdoors when you have finished with your observations. Be sure the weather is hospitable. Suitable locations to place the worms would be a flower bed or garden after a rain.

Kim Davison, Lincoln School for International Studies, Kalamazoo, MI inspired this idea.

Log of Worm Observation Chamber

	Date	Burrows	Animals	Moisture	Odor	Other
Observation # 1						
Observation # 2						
Observation # 3						

Directions

Read *What to look for* . . . below. Record date and observations in the log.
(Hint: List number and length of burrows, number and types of animals.)

- Presence of other animals *(sow bugs, ants, others)*
- Moisture on glass, dampness of leaves
- Changes in mixing of horizons, sand marker
- Worm sightings
- Presence of tunnels
- Presence of food scraps, mold
- Surface area for air exchange *(every tunnel creates more area for air exchange)*
- Aerobic decomposition
- Odor *(earthy, sticky, yucky?)*

What to Look for in the Worm Observation Chamber

Bonus Activity How fast does water move from top to bottom? Pour a small amount in top of chamber and measure time it takes to get to bottom.

> ### Wormformation
> Worms make burrows in more than one way. A worm will push its pointed anterior into a narrow space between soil particles. It then contracts its long muscles, causing the worm to swell up and push grains of soil closer together. The worm repeats this many times, creating a tunnel for it to move in. Another way a worm creates a burrow is to eat its way through the soil. Mucus from the worm cements soil particles together to help retain the burrow's shape.

Purpose

   The activity allows for observation of different kinds of worms and their burrows in soil.

Materials

   - Three different kinds of earthworms (for example, nightcrawler, redworm, and garden worm)
   - Soil Profile Chamber with rocks, moist organic layers and subsoil

Directions

   1. First, construct the Soil Profile box, page 163, as the basis for the Worm Observation Chamber.
   2. Place one of three kinds of worms each week in the Worm Observation Chamber, page 117, over a three week period. After you add the worm to the chamber, record name of worm and date in a Worm Record box below.
   3. Observe each worm and its burrow. Draw a picture of what you see each week in the box below. *Don't forget to feed the worms each week.*
   4. Make a new drawing each week on separate sheets of paper.
   5. At the end of 3 weeks, use the Observation Chart, page 161, to describe in words your observations and conclusions.

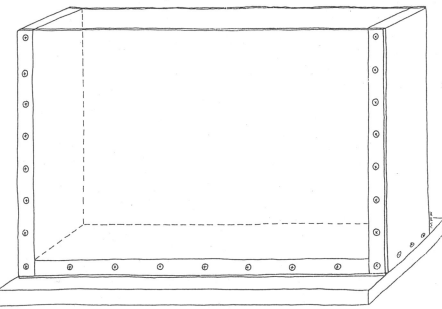

Bonus Activity

   Use a ruler to measure the depth of the burrow starting at the top of the chamber. Label the drawings.

One way to classify earthworms is by where they live and what they do. Three such classes are *epigeic, endogeic, and diageic.*

Wormformation

Epigeic worms live mainly in the organic layer on top of the soil. They can be found where manure is stored on soil. They also live along streams where decaying plant life accumulates, and in compost or piles of damp leaves. The manure worm is a worm which crawls and feeds on the earth's surface. Epigeic earthworms can burrow into soil, but prefer to slither in and out of spaces between organic material in the O (organic) soil horizon. They process large amounts of organic material by eating microorganisms and producing worm castings. This recycles nutrients back into the soil for plants and animals.

Endogeic worms live within the mineral soils beneath the organic layer. They are true tunnelers. Their habitat is usually an inch or more below the soil surface. They commonly occur within the two mineral horizons of soil, the A (topsoil) and B (subsoil) layers. The worms you would most likely find in your garden are endogeic. Their networks of tunnels extend horizontally and at an angle to the soil surface. Endogeic worms make channels for air. The channels also allow for rainwater and melting snow to seep into the soil.

Diageic worms are the deep burrowers. They burrow throughout the depth of the soil. Their long-term habitat may be near parent rock beneath the A and B horizons of soil. Nightcrawlers are diageic earthworms. Their burrows may be several feet deep. They go way down when the weather is so cold that they would freeze, or so dry that they would die from lack of moisture. Diageic worms mix soil layers by dragging organic material into their burrows and by carrying subsoil layers up toward the surface.

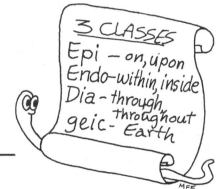

3 CLASSES
Epi — on, upon
Endo — within, inside
Dia — through, throughout
geic — Earth

Directions

Read Wormformation and fill out the chart in words and phrases.

Type of Worm	Worm's Work	Importance to a Healthy Earth

Bonus Activity Draw and label a soil profile chart. Include the three classes of worms in the correct soil layers.

Worms Wanted

Directions

Match the most qualified applicant in Work Wanted with the job in Help Wanted. Draw a line from each Work Wanted ad to the most likely Help Wanted ad.

Work Wanted	Help Wanted
1. Looking for job on construction ground crew. Will work below the surface day or night shifts. Contact: The Dew Worm	**A.** Applications are being accepted for an earth mover. Must be able to transport your weight in soil. Call 555-1234
2. Air ducts specialist looking for work in Great Lakes area. Will relocate on damp nights only. Write: The Pasture Worm	**B.** Need inhabitants for our classroom bin. Room and board are provided. The first 1500 applicants will be considered. Contact Principal Jones.
3. Will take the dirty jobs! No toxic waste, please. Able to lift heavy materials. Call: A. caliginosa	**C.** Entry level positions. Need laborers to dig tunnels for the county. Come in worm or in person to get more information.
4. Want factory work in an expanding industry. Call 555-8765. Ask for "Garbagemouth"	**D.** Babysitter needed. Must have excellent references and experience with cocoons and hatchlings. Send photo.
5. Couple to live in and care for your offspring. Write to The Brandlings.	**E.** Alluring applicants wanted to entice our clients. Call the State Fish Hatchery.
6. Will help attract customers to your agency. Must have life insurance benefits. Contact: L. terrestris	**F.** Full time production worker wanted for a growing waste disposal company. Please slither in for an interview.
7. Want work demonstrating composting techniques. Must provide housing. Call/write: The Redworm	**G.** Air conditioning company desperately seeking ventilation expert to open new territory in the southwest.

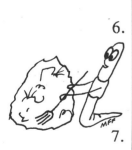

B	D	F	H	J	L	N	P	R	C	T	V	X	Z	A	C	E
A	B	G	I	K	M	O	Q	C	O	C	O	O	N	W	U	W
Y	E	A	R	T	H	W	O	R	M	A	X	C	E	O	I	K
M	O	R	C	P	Q	A	R	S	P	U	Y	W	Y	R	D	F
H	J	L	A	T	N	T	G	R	O	W	G	P	R	M	V	E
X	B	P	D	T	E	E	A	F	S	H	E	J	L	B	P	L
R	E	T	L	V	E	R	N	X	T	Z	N	A	D	I	J	G
R	M	P	S	A	V	Y	I	B	E	G	K	M	M	N	Q	G
T	W	Z	A	D	N	G	C	A	S	T	I	N	G	R	J	I
L	M	P	S	V	N	T	B	O	E	H	K	L	A	P	O	R
I	H	A	T	C	H	L	I	N	G	S	B	U	R	R	O	W
O	T	U	W	A	D	I	G	N	I	O	D	E	B	G	H	A
S	L	I	M	E	M	M	N	T	V	R	B	E	A	Z	T	O
A	M	Q	R	U	V	E	L	P	Q	H	J	T	G	T	A	D
O	J	K	M	N	S	M	O	I	S	T	U	R	E	V	W	R

Directions

Find and circle each word from the Word List in the puzzle above. Cross out each word in the list below as you find it. You will need to look across, up, down, backwards, forwards, and diagonally to find all of the words. We have circled the first word for you. (*Hint: Use a ruler on the diagonal lines of letters to help spot words.*)

Word List

aerate	humus
bacteria	lime
bedding	moisture
burrow	organic
casting	oxygen
cocoon	~~paper~~
compost	plant
earthworm	slime
eat	soil
garbage	water
grow	worm
hatchling	wormbin
	wriggle

Name_____

A	B	C
D	E	F
G	H	I

•J	K•	L•
•M	N•	O•
.P	Q.	R.

S / T / U / V (X pattern)

W / X / Y / Z (X pattern with dots)

Directions

Use the secret code above to decode the interesting facts about worms below.
(*Hint: The title of this page is coded for you.*)

1.

2.

3.

4.

Bonus Activity Use the secret code to write messages to your friends.

> Worms work in ways to break down our food wastes. They clean up our environment. Worm castings are food for plants. We eat vegetable plants grown on the castings. This process is nature's way of recycling.
> **Wormformation**

Directions
Write words or phrases about worms and their work. Begin each one with a letter from the title of this book. A few are started for you.

W iggly worms work in the soil._____

O_____

R_____

M_____

S limy worms slither to find food._____

E_____

A_____

T_____

O_____

U_____

R_____

G arbage makes me think about worms._____

A_____

R_____

B_____

A_____

G_____

E_____

Beyond the Bin

Learner Outcomes

After completing the activities in this unit, the student will:

- understand the relationship between worms and organic waste mangement

- understand the importance of recycling

- understand ways to save the earth's resources and create a better environment

Water is sometimes called the universal solvent because so many different kinds of substances dissolve in it. Water in a worm bin is full of dissolved nutrients that will feed plants. When a worm bin gets too moist, the water which settles in the bottom becomes a dark, murky solution that can be used for watering plants. Some people call this liquid "castings tea" because it is made by soaking worm castings in water. Drier worm bins can yield "castings tea" by placing castings in a screened funnel over a jar and pouring water through them.

Wormformation

Materials
- 9 recycled polystyrene cups or half-pint milk cartons
- shallow box, 2-3 inches deep
- aluminum foil or plastic sheet
- tomato seeds
- garden or flower bed soil
- measuring cup
- 3 containers for liquids
- bulb baster or ladle

Directions

Follow these steps to see if the presence of castings tea makes plants grow better.

1. Punch holes in the bottom of cups.
2. To keep water from leaking, line a shallow box with aluminum foil or sheet of plastic. Place cups in three rows inside the box.
3. Place equal amounts of moist garden or flower bed soil in each cup.
4. Plant 2-3 seeds about 1/4 inch deep in each cup. Cover all the cups with a wet newspaper. Check cups daily until the seeds sprout then remove cover. (Seeds sprout in about 3 days if temperature in the cups is 65° - 70° F.) If more than one plant sprouts per cup, pull out all but the strongest looking.
5. Remove castings tea from bottom of worm bin with a bulb baster or ladle. Mix a different watering solution in each container. (See the "recipes" in the drawing below.)
6. Water each row of seedlings as needed with a different solution using the same amount of liquid for each plant.
7. Record your observations once a week for 4 weeks on the Observation Chart, page 161.

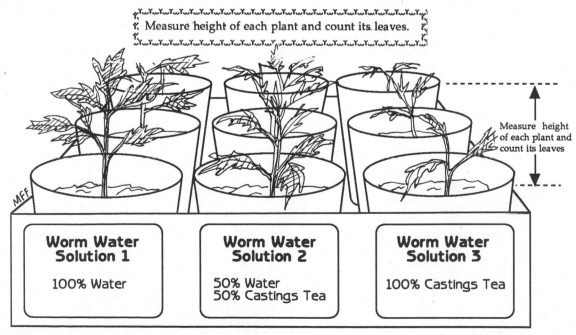

Measure height of each plant and count its leaves.

Measure height of each plant and count its leaves

Worm Water Solution 1 — 100% Water

Worm Water Solution 2 — 50% Water 50% Castings Tea

Worm Water Solution 3 — 100% Castings Tea

Wormformation

Plant seedlings need light, nutrients, and water to grow. Their tiny, hair-like roots drink in nitrogen, phosphorus, and other minerals that are in a water solution. Worm castings and worm "castings tea" are also nutrient sources for plants. In nature, worms line their burrows with nutrient-rich castings, or manure. When plants send their roots into worm burrows they find nutrients to help them grow. Because castings which come through the tiny digestive tract of the worm are so small, the worm's manure is just what a tiny new plant needs.

Materials
- 9 recycled polystyrene cups or half-pint milk cartons
- shallow box, 2-3 inches deep
- tomato seeds
- 3 mixing bowls
- worm castings
- aluminum foil or plastic sheet
- newspaper
- garden or flower bed soil
- peat moss
- sand

Directions

Set up this experiment to see what soil mixture(s) plants like best.

1. Punch holes in the bottom of cups.
2. To keep water from leaking, line a shallow box with aluminum foil or sheet of plastic. Place cups in three rows inside the box.
3. Mix a different soil mixture in each of the three bowls. (See the "recipes" in the drawing below.)
4. Place soil mix A in row one, soil mix B in row two, and soil mix C in row three.
5. Plant 2-3 seeds about 1/4 inch deep in each cup then water and cover all cups with a wet newspaper until the first seeds sprout. Check daily for sign of seeds sprouting. If more than one seed sprouts in each cup, pull out all but the strongest looking sprout. (Sprouting takes place in about three days if the temperature in the cups is 65° - 70° F.)
6. Water each plant regularly with the same amount of water per cup.
7. Record your observations once a week for 4 weeks on the Observation Chart, page 161.

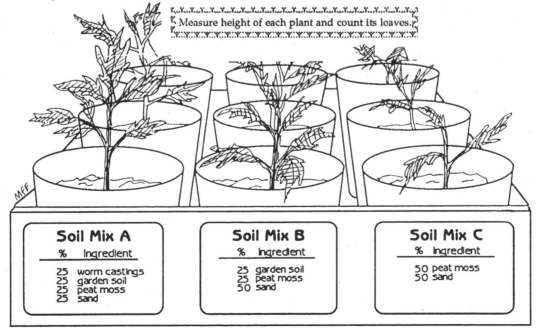

Measure height of each plant and count its leaves.

Soil Mix A		Soil Mix B		Soil Mix C	
%	Ingredient	%	Ingredient	%	Ingredient
25	worm castings	25	garden soil	50	peat moss
25	garden soil	25	peat moss	50	sand
25	peat moss	50	sand		
25	sand				

Tiny Root Song

Tiny Roots

Tiny roots grow where they please,
Into worm burrows with millipedes.

Chorus:
(one clap) Tiny roots   Down, down, down they grow!

Tiny roots suck up the rain,
grow long and deep in worm domain.

Tiny roots grow tall green plants,
above the earth among the ants.

Tiny roots make tiny toys,
for baby sow bugs and nematodes.

Tiny roots with much good sense,
search through the soil for nutrients.

Rain dissolves the rocks in time
and tiny roots come there to dine.

Tiny Roots

Music by Mary Appelhof

Lyrics by Mary Frances Fenton

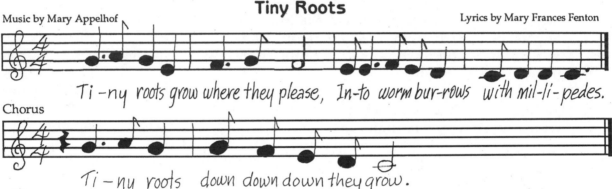

Ti-ny roots grow where they please, In-to worm bur-rows with mil-li-pedes.

Chorus

Ti-ny roots down down down they grow.

Directions

Write the words to a song about the earth. First write down rhyming words such as *soil, toil, foil, boil.* Then use some of the words to rhyme with the last word of each two line lyric. Share your song with a friend.

Rhyming Words

_____
Song Title

_____

_____

_____

_____

_____

_____

_____

Bonus activity   Teach the song *Tiny Roots* to friends.

Wormformation

When vegetable wastes decompose and are eaten by worms, castings are produced. Castings are the worms' manure. The roots of young plants can easily feed on the moist nutrients found in castings. Garden soil also has many minerals that plants need to complete their life cycle. By adding worms and their castings to soil, plants have more kinds of nutrients available to help them grow and produce fruit. Healthy plants are less likely to be attacked and damaged by insects and fungi. They also produce more fruit and seed.

Materials

- 2-liter plastic bottle
- scissors
- measuring cup and spoons
- 6" X 16" construction paper, dark color to keep out light
- masking tape or stapler

- 1/2 cup chopped, vegetable waste
- 2 cups moist, shredded newspaper
- 1T oatmeal or oatbran
- 1 t garden or flower bed soil
- 5 redworms, variety of lengths
- small seeds to sprout (lentils, mung beans, or alfalfa)
- water

Directions

This is a <u>one week</u> observation activity. Follow the steps to make a Garbage Garden and to observe the interaction among plants, worms, and their environment. *(Hint: At the end of observations, return contents and worms to garden, flower bed, or worm bin.)*

1. Soak seeds in water for two days to help them sprout before setting up the Garbage Garden.
2. Cut off the rounded top of a 2-liter bottle. Remove cap.
3. Mix 1 T oatmeal, 1 t soil, 1/2 cup chopped vegetable waste, and moist, shredded newspaper.
4. Place worms, moistened ingredients, and seeds in bottle.
5. Place bottle top back on the bottle to reduce loss of moisture yet let in air. Observe for one week.
6. To keep light away from worms, tape or staple dark paper loosely around bottle. You can easily remove it for observations.
7. Use the Observation Chart, page 161 to record your observations on two different days during a one week period.

Garbage Garden

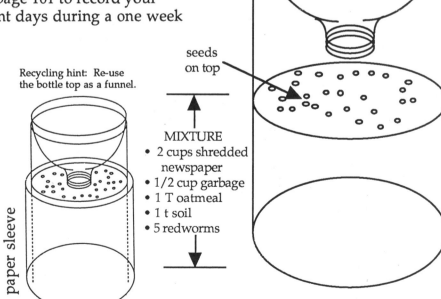

seeds on top

MIXTURE
- 2 cups shredded newspaper
- 1/2 cup garbage
- 1 T oatmeal
- 1 t soil
- 5 redworms

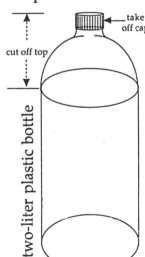

take off cap

cut off top

two-liter plastic bottle

Recycling hint: Re-use the bottle top as a funnel.

paper sleeve

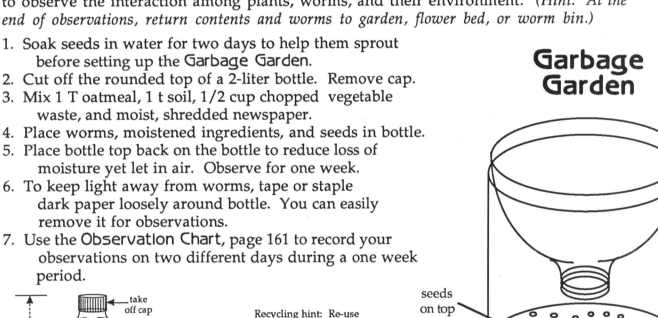

Thanks to Sam Hambly of Camp Allsaw, Downsview, Ont., Canada for this idea.

More Garbage Gardens

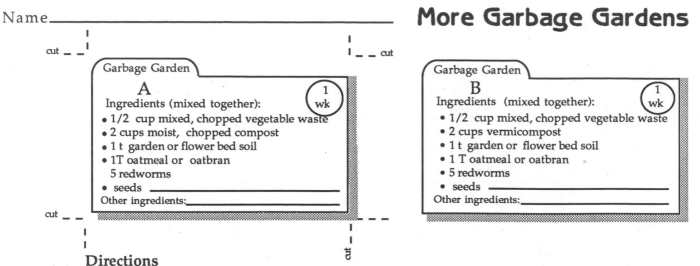

Garbage Garden

A   (1 wk)

Ingredients (mixed together):
- 1/2 cup mixed, chopped vegetable waste
- 2 cups moist, chopped compost
- 1 t garden or flower bed soil
- 1T oatmeal or oatbran
  5 redworms
- seeds _____
Other ingredients:_____

Garbage Garden

B   (1 wk)

Ingredients (mixed together):
- 1/2 cup mixed, chopped vegetable waste
- 2 cups vermicompost
- 1 t garden or flower bed soil
- 1 T oatmeal or oatbran
- 5 redworms
- seeds _____
Other ingredients:_____

Directions

There are many ways to set up your **Garbage Garden**. Make 2 miniature gardens by following the steps on page 129. Soak seeds for two days. Fill each container with a different recipe. Cut out the recipe labels from this page and tape to paper sleeve of each container. Fill the container as labelled. Add other ingredients, if you wish, and record them on the label. Write a description of each ingredient in the recipe <u>before</u> you fill a **Garbage Garden**, then describe each again <u>after</u> one week is up. Describe the worms also. Record your observations on the **Before and After Chart**, page 171. When finished, put all the contents back into a moist garden or worm bin so that the worms will live. *(Hint: See questions bordering the chart.)*

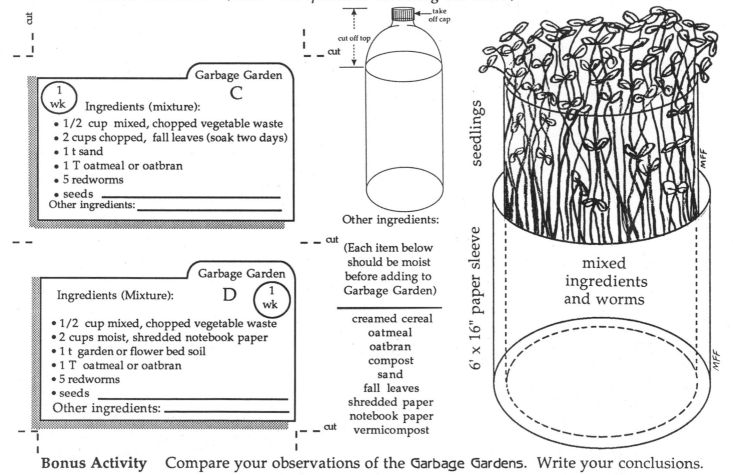

Garbage Garden

C   (1 wk)

Ingredients (mixture):
- 1/2 cup mixed, chopped vegetable waste
- 2 cups chopped, fall leaves (soak two days)
- 1 t sand
- 1 T oatmeal or oatbran
- 5 redworms
- seeds _____
Other ingredients: _____

Garbage Garden

D   (1 wk)

Ingredients (Mixture):
- 1/2 cup mixed, chopped vegetable waste
- 2 cups moist, shredded notebook paper
- 1 t garden or flower bed soil
- 1 T oatmeal or oatbran
- 5 redworms
- seeds _____
Other ingredients: _____

take off cap

cut off top

cut

Other ingredients:

(Each item below should be moist before adding to Garbage Garden)

creamed cereal
oatmeal
oatbran
compost
sand
fall leaves
shredded paper
notebook paper
vermicompost

seedlings

6' x 16" paper sleeve

mixed ingredients and worms

Bonus Activity   Compare your observations of the Garbage Gardens. Write your conclusions.

Thanks to Sam Hambly of Camp Allsaw, Ontario, Canada for this idea.

Vermi Puzzle

Directions

Find the words from the Word List in the diagram below. Words may be forwards, backwards, diagonally forwards, or diagonally backwards. Each word is in a straight line without skipping over letters. Letters can be used more than once. All letters in the diagram will not be used. Circle each word you find and cross off the same word in the Word List. Color in the circled words when you have found them all. If you have done the puzzle correctly, a familiar word will appear.

L	B	Z	W	K	E	M	G	E	D	D	I	C	M	P	O	I	N	T	P	E	S	N	I	D	D	A	B
F	E	M	Y	R	C	R	I	Q	N	E	T	L	G	R	T	C	I	U	K	S	P	I	Z	Z	A	G	I
S	D	M	T	O	L	E	Z	U	A	C	I	D	E	E	T	G	D	B	Q	W	O	R	A	L	N	A	P
M	D	I	R	W	E	F	Z	L	E	J	R	E	N	D	E	N	S	E	W	O	L	I	K	O	W	R	A
U	I	O	O	K	A	L	A	A	R	O	V	P	A	I	M	O	Y	T	U	R	A	N	L	J	U	B	S
I	N	R	V	Y	Q	R	R	X	O	B	Z	O	C	C	R	A	N	L	W	R	N	I	E	H	N	A	C
A	G	D	A	T	U	I	D	D	B	A	W	S	O	T	U	F	E	S	Z	U	I	R	A	A	Y	G	O
T	O	A	W	I	T	F	P	G	I	B	P	I	H	O	V	J	O	H	O	B	Z	O	F	E	X	E	R
M	S	E	R	H	E	X	I	N	C	A	S	T	N	B	X	I	K	Y	S	K	O	P	Q	G	O	K	F

Word List

Four-Letter Words

ACID
EONS
CAST
DRAW
GROW
LEAF
LONG
SOIL
~~TUBE~~
WORK

Five-Letter Words

DENSE
POINT

Seven-Letter Words

AEROBIC
BEDDING
BURROWS
DEPOSIT
GARBAGE
GIZZARD
PREDICT

WORMS EAT OUR GARBAGE Copyright © 1993 Flower Press

Visual Discrimination

Directions
Read this story and answer the questions on Weigh-In Concepts, page 133.

One year I counted and weighed all the earthworms I could hand sort from the top seven inches of a square foot of my garden. I counted 62 worms of all sizes, and at least two species. If I had had an acre under cultivation and if this was, in fact, a representative sample, the total population would have exceeded 2.7 million worms per acre!

These 62 worms weighed two ounces. Extended to one acre, this would give a total weight of 5,445 pounds, or over two and one-half tons of worms in the top seven inches of one acre (43,560 square feet) of soil.

Earthworms of these soil dwelling types eat soil in their search for organic nutrients. This soil is mixed with the organic materials and bacteria in their intestines and is deposited as castings. The weight of these castings per worm per day could easily equal the weight of the worm. To take a conservative figure, let us estimate that the weight of castings deposited per day from one worm is one-eighth the weight of the worm. The total weight of castings produced per acre per day would be 680 pounds. Think of the value to the plants of those castings, and the activity of the worms in producing those castings.

To get an estimate of annual casting production, let us assume that the worms are active only 150 days of the year, giving you 102,093 pounds per year, or over 51 tons of castings per year. (If you have ever tossed a ton of manure onto, and off of a pickup truck, you can begin to appreciate the work worms perform for you in your garden.)

These calculations compare favorably with estimates from scientists around the world. In 1881, Darwin estimated that earthworms deposited from 7 1/2 to 18 tons of casts per acre in pasture. Stockli's work in 1928 comes closer to the figure of 51 tons per acre per year. He estimated that worms produced from 33 to 44 tons per acre in Switzerland.

Estimates from the rich Nile Valley are almost unbelievable. Beaugh estimated that earthworms deposit over 1,000 tons of casts per acre per year. No other area in the world could be expected to exceed the casting production achieved by earthworms in the unusually favorable conditions of the Nile Valley.

The use of chemical fertilizers and pesticides has not only reduced soil earthworm and microbial populations, but also the amounts of natural organic matter present in the soil. These energy-intensive practices have led us to the point where applying greater quantities of fertilizers and pesticides at great expense does less good than the smaller quantities did previously. North temperate climatic regions, especially, could benefit from increased earthworm populations in soils. It is vital to help people understand the advantages of encouraging agricultural practices that increase native earthworm populations in our soils, and to discourage practices that kill them.

from **Worms Eat My Garbage** by Mary Appelhof

Directions
Read the story, *Worm Weigh-In,* on page 132. Answer the questions below.

1. What information is given in the story as evidence to support Mary's estimate that over 2.7 million worms may be found in an acre?

2. The scientific community also uses hectares as a measure of land. A hectare is about 2 1/2 acres. According to Mary's estimates, what would the worm population be in a hectare?

3. In her sample, Mary found 62 worms that weighed two ounces. What was the average weight of a worm?

4. Mary's friend counted 50 worms in the top seven inches of a square foot in his garden. The worms weighed 1 1/2 ounces. What would the total weight of his worms be in one acre?

5. According to the story, what effect do chemical fertilizers and pesticides have on the earth?

6. Why did Mary assume that the worms work only about 150 days in her garden?

Wormformation
Worms live where there is food, moisture, oxygen and a favorable temperature. If these needs are not met they go somewhere else.

Directions

Kirstin, Kenny, and Kim wanted know the average number of worms in their yard and garden. Each person dug up a cubic foot of soil in each of four test sites. Kirstin dug in her organic vegetable garden. Kenny dug his four test sites in the lawn. Kim got permission to dig in a farmer's newly plowed field. They were surprised at what they found. Study the chart below and answer the questions.

Name	Test Site	Number of Worms
Kirstin	A	26
Kirstin	B	12
Kirstin	C	18
Kirstin	D	8
Kenny	E	6
Kenny	F	2
Kenny	G	0
Kenny	H	9
Kim	I	1
Kim	J	0
Kim	K	3
Kim	L	2

1. Find the average number of worms in Kirstin's four test sites.

Answer_____

2. Find the average number of worms in Kenny's test sites.

Answer_____

3. What is the average number of worms in Kim's four test sites?

Answer_____

4. What is the average number of worms for all the test sites?

Answer_____

5. Why you think there were more worms in some test sites than in others?

_____

_____

Name_____   **How Many Worms?**

Directions
Each of the students has a garden. The graph shows the number of worms per square foot each has in his/her garden. Use the graph to answer the questions below.

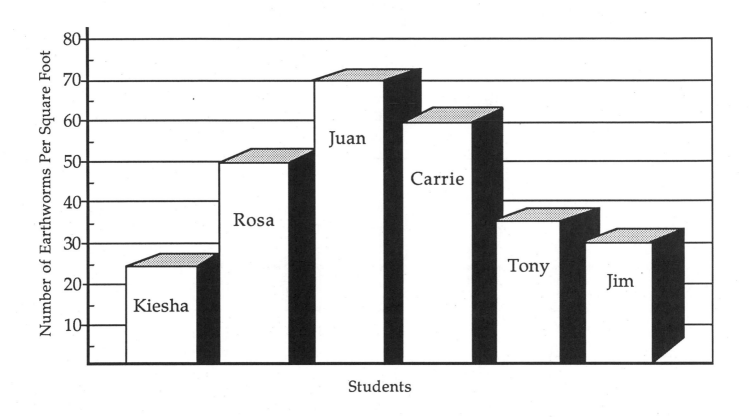

1. Which person has the most worms per square foot? _____

2. Who has the least number of worms per square foot? _____

3. What is the average number of worms per square foot in the gardens of Kiesha, Carrie, and Tony? _____

4. What is the average number of worms per square foot in the gardens belonging to Jim, Juan and Rosa? _____

5. What is the average number of worms per square foot in all the gardens? _____

Bonus Activity Juan's garden is 150 square feet. If the earthworms are evenly distributed in his garden, what is the total number of worms in his garden?

Wormformation

Some scientists have described mass migrations of worms. For unknown reasons, large groups of earthworms come out of their burrows and move to unlikely places. On damp, foggy nights, observers have seen worms slither across sidewalks, crawl up sides of buildings, and even climb up into trees!

Observers give many reasons for this behavior. Some think toxic gases build up in the soil, causing the worms to leave their burrows. Some say that when rain fills up worm burrows it squeezes out all the oxygen. Others say that worms move just because they want to move.

We know that this migration is dangerous for some worms. A worm may get stepped on. Or, when daylight comes, the ultraviolet light from the sun may kill it. Or a worm may dry out.

Directions

Read the Wormformation, answer the questions, and color the numbered boxes below. The correct answer is a word for a place where worms are found.

10	4	6	1	2	12	7	4	10	1	8	7	5	2
8	7	5	10	11	9	5	1	3	6	11	4	10	8
3	4	12	7	8	6	11	12	2	7	5	9	3	11
11	2	3	9	10	7	2	9	11	12	3	4	8	10
10	12	6	4	3	1	4	6	5	9	2	6	1	12

1. Worms migrate during bright sunlight.   *(If true, then color #1; if false, then color #2)*

2. Worms have been found in trees.   *(If true, then color #3; if false, then color #4)*

3. Worms leave their burrows on damp, foggy, nights.   *(If true, color #5; if false, color #6)*

4. Scientists agree on why worms migrate.   *(If true, color #7; if false, color #8)*

5. Ultraviolet light is healthy for worms.   *(If true, color #9; if false, color #10)*

6. Migration can be dangerous for worms.   *(If true, color #11; if false, color #12)*

Bonus Activity Write why you think you find worms on driveways and sidewalks. Read it to a friend.

Directions

Read the poems on this page. Poems are a creative way to share what you know about something. Write a positive poem about worms on the wiggly lines below.
(Hint: Describe where worms live, what they eat, or how you feel about them.)

Worm Woman Rap

If Mary studies worms year after year.
How many worms does she call " dear "?

Try to guess the number,
And if you guess it right.

Ten thousand worms will visit you tonight.
- Mary Frances Fenton

Mr. Owder

Mr. Owder, Mr. Owder, how do you do?
I have a thousand other redworms just like you.
You'll live in my house, snug in your bin
And you'll never go out, 'cause you'll always eat in.
Mr. Owder, Mr. Owder, the earth loves you
For recycling food scraps is the work that you do.
- Barbara Harris

(Do you know what word Mr. Owder
spells backwards?)

Poem Title

What Am I?

When it rains in the spring
And it's night in the town,
I come out of the ground
And wander around.

When daylight comes
If I haven't yet found
My burrow, a rock,
Or a hole in the ground

I dry up and die,
And all you will see
Is a squishy long line
That used to be me.

-Mary Appelhof

Directions
Read each sentence and write the missing word in the boxes to the right. The one-word answers are partly filled in for you. Use the glossary.

Puzzle A

1. Baby worms hatch from a _____   Ⓒ □ c □ □ Ⓝ

2. A stack of leaves and grass clippings is a_____pile. □ o m p o Ⓢ ◯

3. Nutrients provide energy, minerals, and _____   v i t □ m □ n ◯

4. Worms eat _____ matter.   □ r Ⓖ Ⓐ n ◯ c

Puzzle B

1. Worms may freeze at temperatures below___Celsius.   Ⓩ ◯ r o

2. Worms move into burrows to avoid_____   Ⓛ i □ □ t

3. Another word for a worm's manure is _____   Ⓕ □ ◯ e s

4. Worms are sometimes used for _____   b □ Ⓘ Ⓣ

5. Bacteria that need oxygen to stay alive are called____   □ e Ⓡ o □ ◯ c

Bonus Activity Unscramble circled letters to find the two words to complete the sentence below.

Worm _____   _____ plants.
               Puzzle A   Puzzle B

The decompostion of organic matter takes place naturally in woods, meadows, and in your own yard. The process, which takes many months, is aided by heat, moisture, and many kinds of creatures. Gardeners and farmers speed up decompostion by making compost piles. They build a pile by layering materials such as leaves and other plant waste, grass clippings or manure, and water.

Wormformation

Directions

Unscramble the words in the compost pile. Write the correct word under the scrambled word. Words to find are: Air Vent, Manure, Heat, Worm, Centipede, Sow Bug, Leaves, Grass, Vegetable, Fungus, Weeds

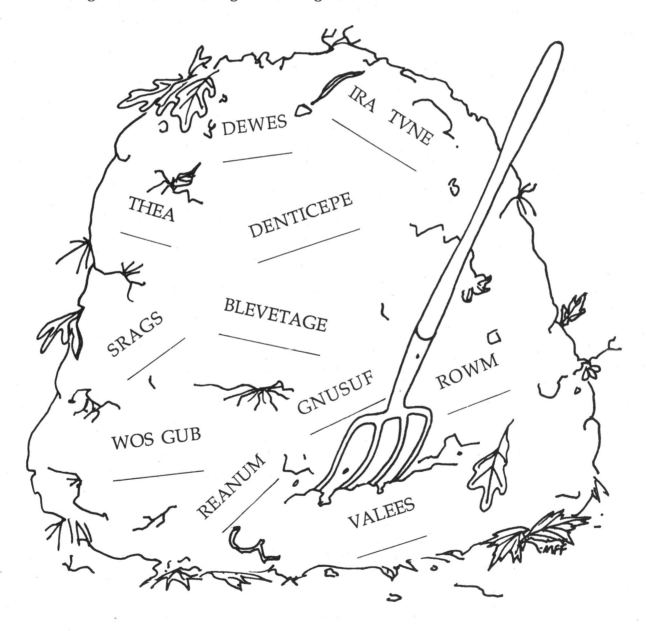

DEWES

IRA TVNE

THEA

DENTICEPE

SRAGS

BLEVETAGE

GNUSUF

ROWM

WOS GUB

REANUM

VALEES

Name_____ **Worm Cartoons**

Directions

Be a cartoonist. Print what you think is being said in the "balloons."   Draw and write your own cartoon in the blank box. *(Hint: Read the ideas written around the edges of this page.)*

I hope beetle stays away from _____.

My babies will grow up to be _____

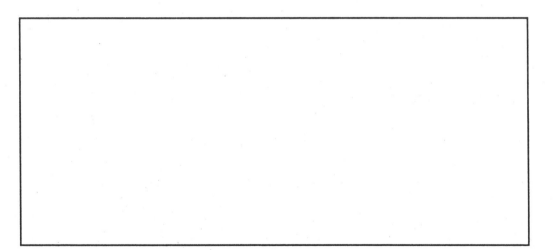

I eat only _____.

What are the names of your twins? _____

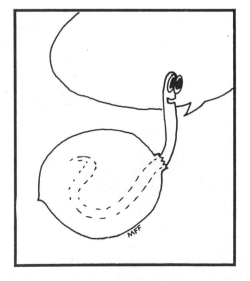

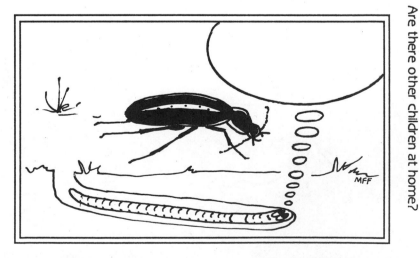

Are there other children at home?

Beetle could give us a ride to _____.   Will you teach my kids to_____?.   Are those real eyes?

WORMS EAT OUR GARBAGE   Copyright © 1993 Flower Press

Creativity/Humor

Compost Cut-Out

1.
Color all the objects and animals around the page.

2.
Draw an outline of a compost pile on 8 " X 8" paper.

3.
Draw wavy lines from top to bottom of drawing. Fold the drawing in half (Fold #1).

4.
Cut along wavy lines on both sides of the folded paper at once. Do <u>not</u> cut across or beyond Folds #2 and #3.

5.
Fold top and bottom of colored paper in the opposite direction from the center fold. Push back every other strip.

6.
Cut out a second sheet of colored paper larger than the first. Fold in half and paste it behind the first sheet.

Fold 3

Fold 1

7.
Cut a strip of paper 1/2" X 5" and glue it to the side of the cut-out so it will hold its shape.

Fold 2

8.
Cut out all the objects and glue them to cut-out.

Materials
- construction paper
- scissors
- glue
- colored pens, pencils, or crayons

Directions
Make a paper cut-out of a compost pile. Use references to identify the objects and animals in your compost pile.

Directions

Recyclers often use many of the terms below. Can you find all of them? Look forwards, backwards, up, down, or diagonally. Look always in a straight line and never skip letters. Circle each term in the diagram, then cross it off in the word list.
(Hint: One is done for you.)

Save the Environment

```
R E D U C E S E N S I B L E
C S A V E L A N D F I L L M
T L C D E R V O R E G O N I
R F E S A V E E N E R G Y C
A B G A H I E N J K E L S H
S O N S N L N M E N C A M I
H T E B M A V O A W Y S A G
W T W E P A I Q S R C S S A
O L S V S T R R Y U L V H N
R E P E A T O T W R E U S E
M S A R J U N K M A I L X W
F T P A L U M I N U M Z F A
O A E G U S E D O I L B U S
O T R E C O N V E N I E N T
D E P O S I T I N C A N S E
```

Word List

ALUMINUM	BOTTLE STATE
CONVENIENT	EASY
GLASS	MICHIGAN
OREGON	~~REDUCE~~
REPEAT	SAVE ENERGY
SAVE LANDFILL	SMART
TIN CANS	USED OIL
BEVERAGE	CLEAN AIR
DEPOSIT	FUN
JUNK MAIL	NEWSPAPER
RECYCLE	RENEW
REUSE	SAVE ENVIRONMENT
SENSIBLE	SMASH
TRASH	WORM FOOD
WASTE	

Name_____

Directions
Find the four errors in each picture.   Write a sentence to describe each error.

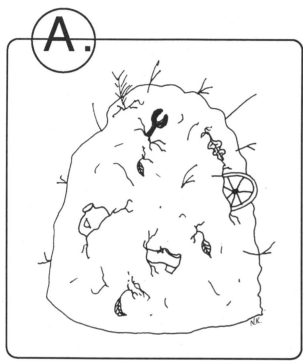

Outdoor Compost Pile

A1. _A metal wrench does not belong in the compost pile._
_____

A2._____
_____

A3._____
_____

A4._____
_____

B1._____
_____
_____

B2._____
_____

B3._____
_____

B4._____
_____
_____

Home Recycling Center

Directions
For one week list the items you throw away in your classroom. Then answer the questions.

Items I've Thrown Away

Monday	_____
	_____
Tuesday	_____
	_____
Wednesday	_____
	_____
Thursday	_____
	_____
Friday	_____
	_____

1. Which of the materials you threw away took up the most space?

2. Describe ways you and your class can recycle some of its trash.

3. Describe ways you and your class can avoid producing some of its trash.

Bonus Activity   Share your findings with friends. Make a chart of the results.

Throwing something away does not make it go away. It just goes somewhere else, such as in a landfill. It is often easier to wash and reuse than to throw an item away, haul it to a dump and bury it, and buy a replacement. It is also better for the environment.

Waste is not Waste until It is Wasted

Directions

Draw a line from each item in the Disposable Products column to the best choice item in the Solutions for a Better Environment column. *(Hint: The first one is done for you.)*

Disposable Products and Packaging	Solutions for a Better Environment
plastic plates	use ceramic coffee mugs and wash
polystyrene cups	use plastic cups and wash
plastic forks, spoons, knives	wash and reuse
plastic cups	buy in bulk and re-package in used containers such as bags and bottles
oatmeal boxes	
tin or aluminum cans	buy in larger quantities
cereal boxes	add to compost pile or worm bin
plastic bags, quart size or less	send to landfill
notebook paper, printed one side	make into crafts projects
table scraps	use back side of paper
bread wrappers	
milk jugs	send to recycling center

Bonus Activity   Draw a picture of a crafts project made out of recycled material. Label it.

Directions

Read the Ad-Information and select an item to sell from the "Products to Sell" list below. List its benefits and design an ad to go into a gardening magazine.

My product is superior because:

_____

_____

My product benefits others in this way:

_____

_____

The difference between my product and the competition's product is:

_____

_____

Ad-Information

A way to sell a product that you think is great is to focus on its good qualities and list its advantages over similar products. Then, show how the user will benefit from using your product. Advertisers like to use large lettering, bright colors, pictures, and motion in their ads to get the attention of the reader. They know that large and colorful things will "catch our eye". Television advertisers know that sound will make us "perk up our ears."

Products to Sell
(Select one)
· worm bin
· worm farm
· recycling labels for recycling bins
· plant fertilizer from worm castings
· flower baskets

My ad looks like this:

Directions

Decode the messages to discover interesting facts about recycling.

```
                          CODE
  A = 1,   B = 2,   C = 3,   D = 4,   E = 5,   F = 6,   G = 7,   H = 8,   I = 9,
  J = 10,  K = 11,  L = 12,  M = 13,  N = 14,  O = 15,  P = 16,  Q = 17,
  R = 18,  S = 19,  T = 20,  U = 21,  V = 22,  W = 23,  X = 24,  Y =25    Z = 26
```

1. 1   16,5,18,19,15,14   16,18,15,4,21,3,5,19   1,2,15,21,20   20,23,15

_____

16,15,21,14,4,19   15,6   7,1,18,2,1,7,5   5,1,3,8   4,1,25.

_____

2. 1,2,15,21,20   6,15,18,20,25   16,5,18,3,5,14,20   15,6   3,21,18,2,19,9,4,5

_____

7,1,18,2,1,7,5   9,19   16,1,16,5,18   16,18,15,4,21,3,20,19.

_____

3.

18,5,3,25,3,12,9,14,7   15,14,5   20,15,14   15,6   14,5,23,19,16,1,16,5,18

_____

19,1,22,5,19   19,5,22,5,14,20,5,5,14   20,18,5,5,19.

_____

Coding

Fact   Organic kitchen waste contaminates recyclables. Worms can eat about 1/2 of their weight in food waste each day. They turn it into nutrient-rich potting soil for growing healthy plants.

Recycling plastic milk jugs saves landfill space and fossil fuels. The plastic in milk jugs can be reground and made into irrigation pipe and high quality, weather-resistant lumber.   **Fact**

Junk mail wastes resources. Because junk mail contains plastic and glues, it is recycled as low-grade mixed paper. To receive less junk mail, have your parents request the Direct Mail Marketing Association to remove their name from lists sold by the major list suppliers.   **Fact**

Recycling aluminum saves energy. Creating a new product from recycled aluminum requires only 4% of the energy needed to produce that product from its ore, bauxite.   **Fact**

Fact   Recycling paper saves forests. Paper products use about 35% of the world's commercial wood harvest.

Directions

Read the **Facts** above. To find the hidden word read each statement below and color the spaces as directed.
(Hint: If you answer correctly, you will spell a color that stands for the wise use of the earth's resources.)

1. If recycling plastic milk jugs saves forests, color the #1 spaces.

2. If recycling aluminum saves energy, color the #2 spaces.

3. If paper products use up 35% of the world's commercial wood harvest, color the #3 spaces.

4. If earthworms recycle organic kitchen waste, color the #4 spaces.

5. If worms eat half their weight in organic waste per day, color the #5 spaces.

6. If junk mail saves resources, color the #6 spaces.

7. If you can get your name removed from junk mail lists, color the #7 spaces.

8. If plastic milk jugs can be reground and made into waterproof lumber, color the #8 spaces.

Bonus Activity

To receive less junk mail, ask the Direct Mail Marketing Association, 6 East 43rd Street, New York, NY 10017 to remove your family's name from lists sold by the major list brokers. Be sure to get permission from your parents or guardians to do this.

Name_____ **Look at Landfills**

A modern landfill is not just a hole in the ground filled with trash. Engineers attempt to design landfills so that water does not leak out. They line the bottom of the landfill with several feet of clay and heavy sheets of plastic. On top of this they place a layer of sand or gravel so that the huge bulldozers do not puncture the lining. Every day dozens of garbage trucks come to the landfill and deposit full loads of trash at the work area. At the end of the day, bulldozers push about 6 inches of subsoil over the trash. Some materials decompose in a landfill, others do not. **Wormformation**

Materials
- large clear container with a lid
- food scraps
- soil and water
- paper scraps
- plastic scraps
- metal scraps

Directions
1) Fill container halfway with soil.

2) Bury the scraps in the soil with scraps near the side of the container.

3) Add 7-15 cm of additional soil on top of the soil with trash scraps. Pack the soil to leave 3 cm of air space on the top.

4) Moisten the soil with water.

5) Record your observations over a 3-week period, and make conclusions about what might decompose in a landfill.

DECOMPOSITION RECORD

	Food Scraps	Paper Scraps	Plastic Scraps	Metal Scraps
Week 1				
Week 2				
Week 3				

Conclusions concerning materials that do and do not decompose:

There once was a large and beautiful city. Its only landfill closed. People had to find other ways to handle their trash. Some adventurous people learned they could set up a wooden bin in their backyard, fill it with moistened newspaper and a pound of redworms, and bury their food waste in the bin. The redworms ate the waste. The adventurers found they could get rid of their garbage, and they could grow delicious vegetables from the worm-worked wastes their worm bin produced. **Wormformation**

Directions

Look up the name and address of a public official in your community who has responsibility for recycling or for handling solid waste. Write a letter explaining the value of worms in your classroom. Invite that person to your class to see your worms at work. Draw a Kids and Worms logo in the box. *(Hint: Use a phone book. Call a city or county office to learn the public official's name and office address.)*

Date _____

Name _____

Title _____

Organization _____

Address _____

City _____ State _____ Zip Code _____

Kids and Worms Logo

Dear _____

_____

_____

_____

_____

_____

_____

_____

Sincerely,

Come see the Worms !

_____
Name

Date _____

_____
Teacher's Name

Time _____

Place _____

Directions

Design a T-shirt that might make your friends and family feel "good" about the work of worms.

Bonus Activity   Describe your T-shirt in words. Tell why you chose your design.

The Worm City

Worm City has over 4,000 worm bins. If each family gets rid of 5 pounds of food waste each week in their worm bin, that would be 20,000 pounds of waste per week. Divided by 2,000 pounds per ton, that is 10 tons of garbage per week. In one year (52 weeks), over 500 tons of garbage is eaten by worms. Since this city spends about $75 per ton to haul and dispose of its garbage, you can say that the worms save the city and its people $31,000 per year.

Wormformation

Directions

Read the Wormformation, and solve the problems below.

Middleview has a population of 987 living in 359 households. Sixty percent of its households have worm bins. It costs $80 per ton to haul and dispose of garbage in Middleview. The average amout of food waste each family gets rid of in worm bins is 5 pounds per week.

1. How much garbage is eaten by worms in one day?

2. How much garbage is eaten by worms in one week?

3. How much garbage is eaten by worms in one year?

4. How much money does Middleview save by using worms?

Imagine that in your city or town, ten percent of the households have worms eat their garbage. The average amount of food waste each family gets rid of in worm bins is 6 pounds per week. (*Hint: Find out the population of your city or town and average number of people per household.*)

1. How much garbage would be eaten in your community by worms in one year?

2. What are the environmental benefits of having worms eat your garbage?

Rules for Brainstorming

Brainstorming is a technique for coming up with many ideas. The rules followed in brainstorming are:

        -one person at a time
        -any ideas OK
        -no criticism
        -lots of ideas
        -crazy ideas OK
        -no right or wrong
        -evaluate ideas later   **Wormformation**

Direction

Read the Wormformation for the rules. Brainstorm as many ideas as you can for each of the categories presented and write them below.

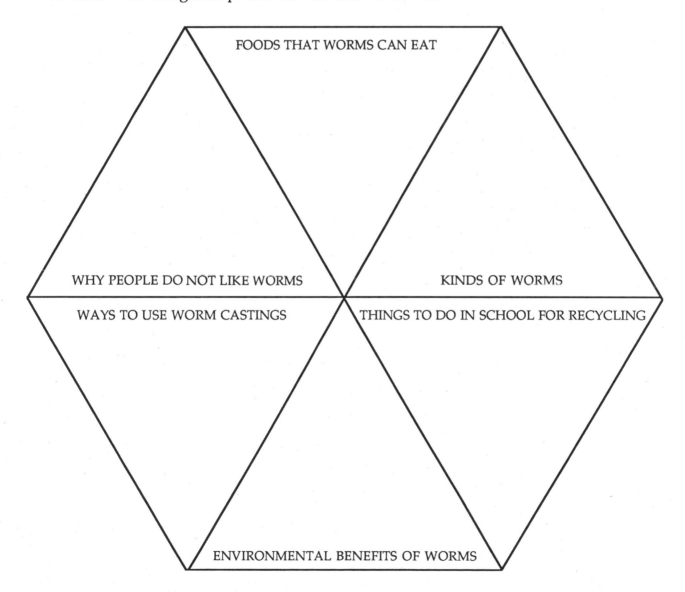

FOODS THAT WORMS CAN EAT

WHY PEOPLE DO NOT LIKE WORMS

KINDS OF WORMS

WAYS TO USE WORM CASTINGS

THINGS TO DO IN SCHOOL FOR RECYCLING

ENVIRONMENTAL BENEFITS OF WORMS

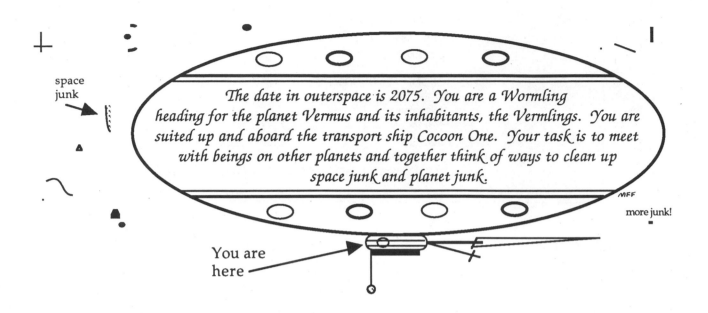

space
junk

You are
here

The date in outerspace is 2075. You are a Wormling heading for the planet Vermus and its inhabitants, the Vermlings. You are suited up and aboard the transport ship Cocoon One. Your task is to meet with beings on other planets and together think of ways to clean up space junk and planet junk.

more junk!

Directions
Answer the questions by writing your ideas for cleaning up the galaxy.

A. *What makes an ideal recycling planet?*_____
_____
_____
_____
_____
_____

B. *What makes the Vermlings and the Wormlings good recyclers?*_____
_____
_____
_____
_____

C. *What can be done to get rid of space junk?*_____
_____
_____
_____
_____
_____

Wormlings' Costumes

Hat
aluminum foil
plastic wrap
plastic packaging

Eyes
hole punch material
seeds
beads
beans
buttons
paper disks

The Spacesuit

Shiny paper
construction paper
cardboard shapes
plastic packaging
tube sections
plastic ring
styrofoam
string
cloth

Directions
Make a worm finger puppet in a space suit. Here are some ideas for materials.

Gift from Wormlings...
wire shapes
beads
metal scraps
paper clip
seeds
written note
tiny picture
tiny object

Noses
rubberband
string
paper tubes
cotton

Tail
Paper roll
cloth
string
rope

Arms
tie twists
pipe cleaners
rolled paper
string

Bonus Activity: Write a script for your puppet. Call the story, "Wormling Meets the Creature," and present it to a young child.

Creativity

Directions
    Be a bumper sticker designer. Create a sticker for each of these clients.

This client wants a bumper sticker with a message about her worm bin. *Make it with Wormpower*	This client wants a bumper sticker that tells about the value of recycling
This client want a bumper sticker with a message about his compost pile.	This client wants a bumper sticker with a message about the value of worms.

WORMS EAT OUR GARBAGE Copyright © 1993 Flower Press

Creativity

> ### Wormformation
> Humor occurs when you put two or more familiar things or situations together in an unusual way. For example, in Lewis Scott's drawings below, the familiar worm has paste-on wings and is flying like a bird. Bird wings are also familiar to us, but they seem odd on a worm. The caption provides new meaning by linking the bird and worm together in an absurd or ridiculous way.

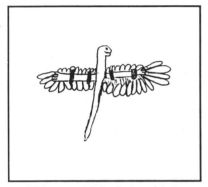

This one thinks he's a bird so he won't get eaten.

This one thinks he's a woodpecker.

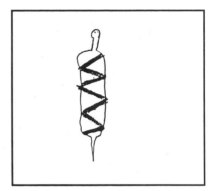

This one went through rush hour.

Reprinted with permission by Peter Avram, Estabrook/New Horizon School, Ypsilanti, Michigan

Directions
Read the **Wormformation** and study the cartoons above. Draw three or more different worms doing something funny. Write a caption for each drawing.

Bonus Activity Make a book cover for your drawings and share with a friend.

Notes

Appendix A
Charts and Record Sheets

Project Planning Calendar

This calendar lists the number of days from the beginning of the year to any particular date. Its purpose is to help you determine experiment starting and ending dates and days when action needs to be taken. To use:

1. Find the number for the day you start your project. For example, if you start the project on **February 10**, look down the **Day of the Month** column to find **10**. Now look across to the **February** column and find **Day 41**.
2. If you want to look at your experiment in 30 days, add 30 days to **Day 41**, giving you **Day 71**.
3. To find the day and month of **Day 71** on the chart, look up the column to find the month and look across to find **Day 12** in the **Day of the Month** column.
4. The chart tells you to look at your experiment again on **Mar. 12**.

Day of Month	Jan	Feb	Mar	Apr	May	Jun	Jul	Aug	Sep	Oct	Nov	Dec
1	1	32	60	91	121	152	182	213	244	274	305	335
2	2	33	61	92	122	153	183	214	245	275	306	336
3	3	34	62	93	123	154	184	215	246	276	307	337
4	4	35	63	94	124	155	185	216	247	277	308	338
5	5	36	64	95	125	156	186	217	248	278	309	339
6	6	37	65	96	126	157	187	218	249	279	310	340
7	7	38	66	97	127	158	188	219	250	280	311	341
8	8	39	67	98	128	159	189	220	251	281	312	342
9	9	40	68	99	129	160	190	221	252	282	313	343
10	10	41	69	100	130	161	191	222	253	283	314	344
11	11	42	70	101	131	162	192	223	254	284	315	345
12	12	43	71	102	132	163	193	224	255	285	316	346
13	13	44	72	103	133	164	194	225	256	286	317	347
14	14	45	73	104	134	165	195	226	257	287	318	348
15	15	46	74	105	135	166	196	227	258	288	319	349
16	16	47	75	106	136	167	197	228	259	289	320	350
17	17	48	76	107	137	168	198	229	260	290	321	351
18	18	49	77	108	138	169	199	230	261	291	322	352
19	19	50	78	109	139	170	200	231	262	292	323	353
20	20	51	79	110	140	171	201	232	263	293	324	354
21	21	52	80	111	141	172	202	233	264	294	325	355
22	22	53	81	112	142	173	203	234	265	295	326	356
23	23	54	82	113	143	174	204	235	266	296	327	357
24	24	55	83	114	144	175	205	236	267	297	328	358
25	25	56	84	115	145	176	206	237	268	298	329	359
26	26	57	85	116	146	177	207	238	269	299	330	360
27	27	58	86	117	147	178	208	239	270	300	331	361
28	28	59	87	118	148	179	209	240	271	301	332	362
29	29		88	119	149	180	210	241	272	302	333	363
30	30		89	120	150	181	211	242	273	303	334	364
31	31		90		151		212	243		304		365

Observation Chart

_____
Name

Time and Date of Observations

Date _____ Time _____	Date _____ Time _____	Date _____ Time _____

Items to Observe

Conclusions _____

_____

_____

_____

_____

_____

_____

Worm Bin Set Up

Worm Bin Size _____

Lb of Worms _____

Lb of Bedding _____

Lb of Water _____

Lb of Food _____

Worm Bin Record

_____

Set Up Date

Burying Locations

1	2	3
6	5	4
7	8	9

Date	Ounces of Garbage	Temp Room	Bin	Burying Location	Comments

Total calendar days _____ Total oz _____ Total lb _____ Total weeks _____ Average oz per day _____ Average lb per week _____

HOW TO BUILD A WORM AND SOIL PROFILE OBSERVATION CHAMBER

Background Information

Left undisturbed for a long time, soil forms layers known as soil horizons. Each horizon has certain characteristics distinguished not only by position, but by color, amount of organic matter, and presence of living organisms. Cutting into an area of undisturbed land, such as when a road is cut through a hill, exposes these layers. A photograph, drawing, or other graphic representation of these horizontal layers is called a soil profile.

This model serves three purposes: (1) to graphically demonstrate a soil profile, (2) to facilitate the observation of worms, and (3) to study the effects on soil of different types of worms, such as redworms, garden worms, or nightcrawlers.

Materials

2   12" x 18" sheets of acrylic plastic
    (have an 18" x 24" sheet cut in half)
2   12" 1 x 4 lumber
1   16 1/2" 1 x 4 lumber
1   18" 1 x 6 lumber
48   3/4" Phillips round-head
    machine screws
10   1 1/4" wood screws (size 8)
1   white candle

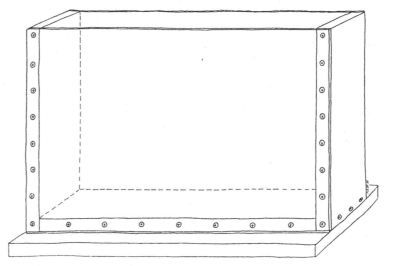

Tools

Drill with 1/8" bit
Phillips screwdriver

Directions

1. Rub the candle on all surfaces of the wood using pressure. This will help waterproof and protect the wood.

2. Placing the 16 1/2" base between the sides, use three 1 1/2" screws to fasten each side to the base. Take care to position the sides at right angles to the base.

3. Place the acrylic sheet in position on the frame and drill holes through the acrylic and into the wood for securing the acrylic onto the base. Insert screws on the bottom of the frame prior to drilling the sides and placing the screws.

4. To stabilize the unit, attach the 6" board to the base with the remaining wood screws. Counter sink the holes so that the screws do not scratch the tabletop when the chamber is in its upright position.

See How to Set Up a Soil Profile, *page 114, and* How to Set Up and Maintain a Worm Observation Chamber, *page 117, for instructions on how to set up the contents and use the soil profile and worm observation chamber.*

Daily and Weekly Progress Chart

_____
Name

	Week No. _____	Week No. _____	Week No. _____
Monday			
Tuesday			
Wednesday			
Thursday			
Friday			

	Week ___	Week ___	Week ___	Week ___	Week ___	Week ___	Week ___	Week ___
Monday								
Tuesday								
Wednesday								
Thursday								
Friday								

Decomposition Record Sheet

_____
Name

Directions Write the name of the item observed above each circle with lines.

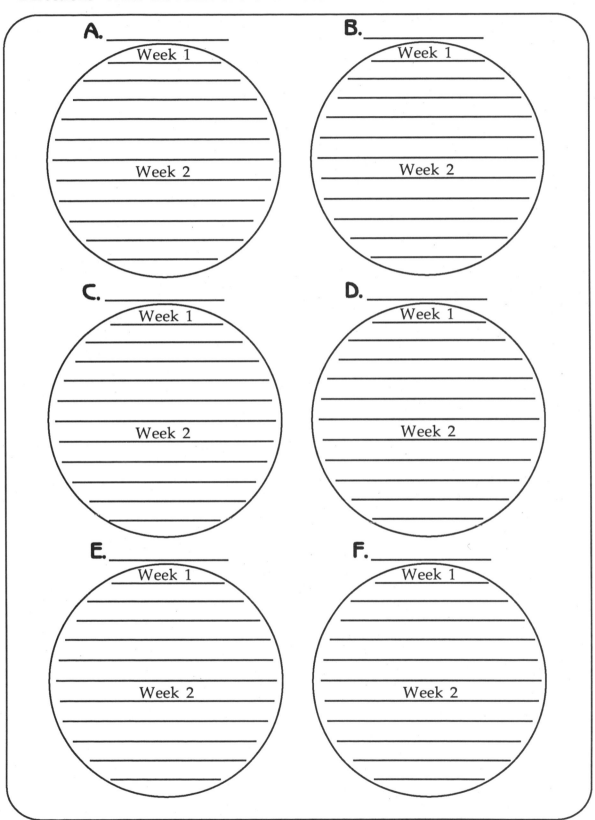

A. _____
Week 1
Week 2

B. _____
Week 1
Week 2

C. _____
Week 1
Week 2

D. _____
Week 1
Week 2

E. _____
Week 1
Week 2

F. _____
Week 1
Week 2

WORMS EAT OUR GARBAGE   Copyright © 1993   Flower Press

Recording Observations

The Answer Post

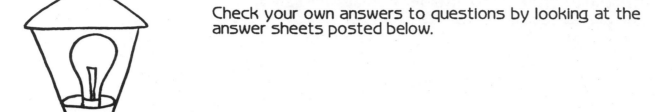

Check your own answers to questions by looking at the answer sheets posted below.

Task Planning Sheet

_____
Name of Event

_____
Date of Event

Tasks to do	Person in Charge	Date Due

Metric Conversion Charts

The multiplication factors in this chart have been rounded to two decimals places. The conversions you find are approximations.

When you know . . .	Multiply by . . .	To find . . .
Length		
millimeters	0.04	inches
centimeters	0.39	inches
meters	3.28	feet
meters	1.09	yards

	Length	
inches	25.40	millimeters
inches	2.54	centimeters
feet	30.48	centimeters
yards	0.91	meters

	Area	
square centimeters	0.16	square inches
square meters	1.20	square yards

	Area	
square inches	6.45	square centimeters
square feet	0.09	square meters
square yards	0.84	square meters

	Mass/Weight	
grams	0.035	ounce
kilograms	2.21	pounds

	Mass/Weight	
ounces	28.35	grams
pounds	0.45	kilograms

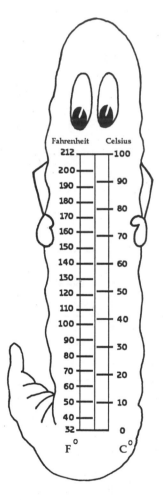

WORMS EAT OUR GARBAGE Copyright © 1993 Flower Press

Metric Conversion Chart

Game Cards/ Question Cards

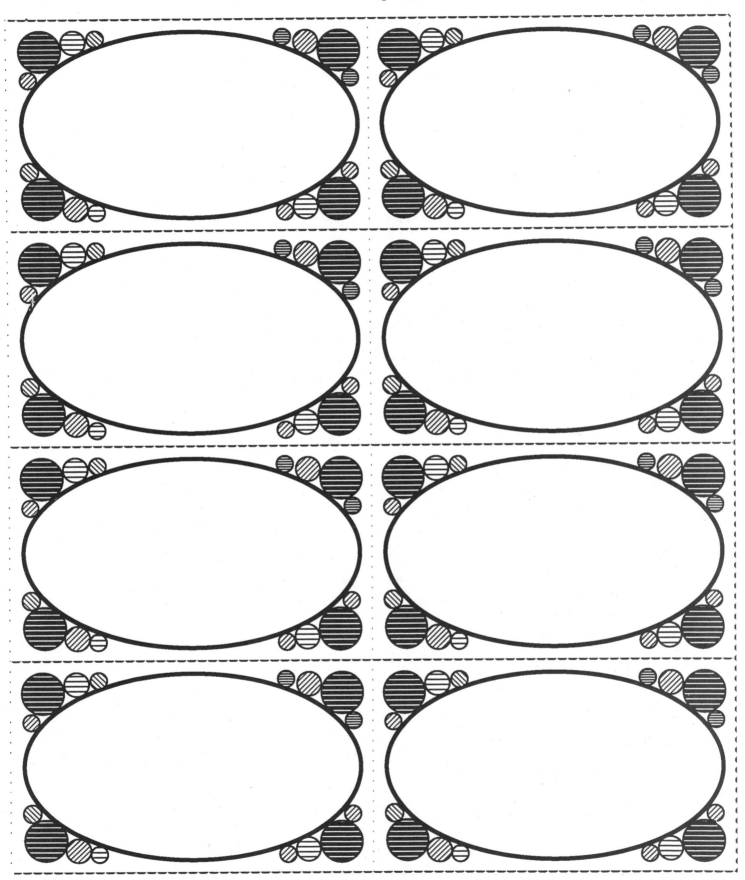

WORMS EAT OUR GARBAGE Copyright © 1993 Flower Press

Blank Card Set

Worms Eat Our Garbage

Certificate of Recognition

presented to

_____

for

_____

*Given at*_____ *this*____ *day of*_____ , ____.

_____

Signature

_____   _____
Your Name   Name of object to observe

Before and After Chart

Before

I observed the following: _____

_____
_____
_____
_____
_____
_____
_____
_____
_____
_____
_____
_____
_____
_____
_____
_____

After

I observed the following: _____

_____
_____
_____
_____
_____
_____
_____
_____
_____
_____

Soil Profile Observation Chart

_____
Name

Directions

Starting with layer #1, write your description of each layer of the soil profile. _(Hint: See the ideas on the borders of this page.)_

Names of soil layers (horizons)

Size of rocks

Layer #5
_____
_____
_____
_____

Layer #4
_____
_____
_____
_____

Color of layers

Layer #3
_____
_____

Texture

Layer #2
_____
_____
_____
_____

Layer #1
_____
_____
_____
_____
_____

Smell

Volume of each layer

Appendix B

Answers and Ideas
(Teacher Pages)

Bulletin Board Ideas

1.

CLASSROOM WASTE STREAM

Re-use
Landfill
Bags
Plastics
organics
OUR CLASS
Recycle
Bulk Food Reduce
Paper
glass Plastic

1. Display objects from classroom waste stream.
2. Display student papers and projects.
3. Present art and ideas.
4. Create a collage of food pictures from magazines.
5. Mural serves as backdrop for charts and graphs.

2.

Hatching New Ideas

3.

WORM Badges and Bumper Stickers

WORM POWER

HONK IF YOU LOVE worms

4.

FEED US

5.

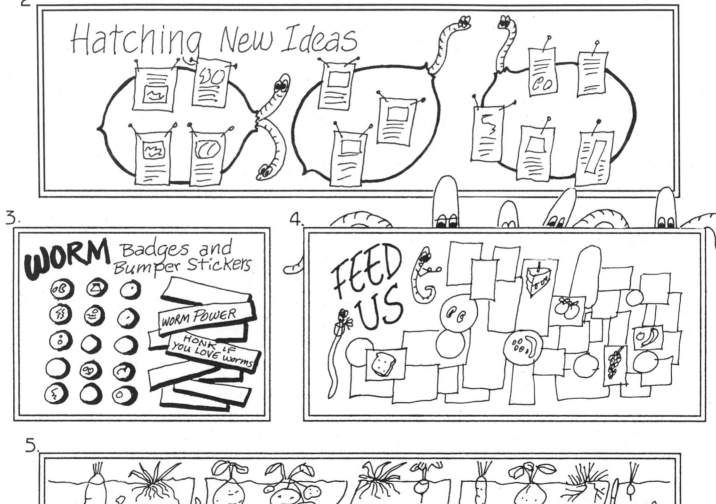

Graph

Chart

ART

PICTURE

PHOTO

ANSWER POST

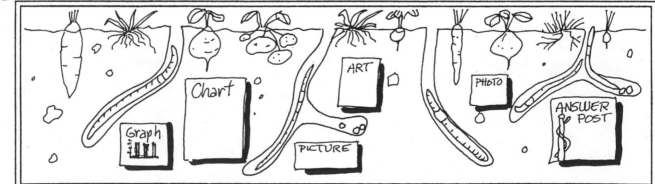

WORMS EAT OUR GARBAGE Copyright © 1993 Flower Press

Bulletin Board Ideas

ANSWERS AND IDEAS

General Ideas

References

Provide references for additional information to complete activity pages. Suggestions include: a dictionary, a thesaurus, an encyclopedia, Worms Eat My Garbage, copies of the Glossary, and other selected references (list included in this book).

With or Without a Worm Bin

Not all activities require a worm bin. You can purchase worms for observation and experimentation from worm growers or bait shops. Depending on time of year and locale, you can collect worms from the "wild."

Post the Answers

Answers for most activity pages are included in this section. Post answers in the classroom so students may evaluate their own products.

Vocabulary

Technical terms specifically related to worms and vermicomposting are defined in the book's Glossary. The content of many activities provide sources for general vocabulary development. Present difficult words and their definitions to students when introducing each activity.

Reproducible Forms

Student recording forms are found in the Appendices. These reproducible forms are needed to complete a variety of activities in this book. Instructions on the activity pages will direct you to the appropriate form(s). Because the forms are relatively generic, use them in other learning experiences where students are required to document their observations.

Sequenced Activities

The activities are sequenced within units according to content. The teacher may want to review each unit and select activities that meet the needs of students and the sequence of instruction.

Level of Difficulty

Activities in this book range in difficulty level from simple to complex, from Grade 4 to Grade 8+. The teacher is encouraged to modify the activities to meet the student's ability and skill levels.

Background Information/Content

The background information needed to complete the activities is included in the Wormformation section on the activity page and in the following Specific Answers and Ideas section.

Measurement Abbreviations

Like many writers of scientific subjects, we chose not to use periods with measurement abbreviations unless they spell words, as in in. (inches). We used the singular form for both singular and plural forms

Create-A-Center

Create a special place in your classroom to house your worm bin and related resources. Some of the materials you can include in the worm center are:

- worm bin
- reusable plastic or rubber gloves
- tweezers and/or toothpicks
- paper towels
- trays and muffin pans
- petri dishes
- magnifying glasses and/or microscope
- garden fork
- weighing balance or scale
- thermometer
- plastic pails, plastic or glass bottles and jars
- rulers
- stop watch, digital watch, or watch with second hand
- flashlight
- measuring cups and spoons
- cellophane (yellow, blue, red, and green)
- cardboard
- reference books and materials

Encourage students to think of a clever title for your center. We welcome pictures of your worm center!

Specific
Answers and Ideas

Page 1
Answers - 1. long and thin 2. no 3. yes 4. mouth
5. no 6. anterior 7. posterior 8. clitellum
9. segment 10. setae

Page 5
Answers - 1. *Lumbricus terrestris* 2. redworm
3. woodlands 4. 144 - 585 cm 5. 3.2 - 5.6 in.
6. *Lumbricus terrestris* or nightcrawler.

Page 6
Answers - 1. animal 2. animal 3. mineral
4. mineral 5. mineral 6. mineral 7. animal
8. mineral 9. plant 10. animal

Page 7
Answers - 1. earthworms move by themselves
2. answers will vary 3. answers will vary; general
ideas: in search of food and to avoid danger 4. skin
is moist 5. long and thin

Page 8
Answers - 1. *Lumbricus terrestris* 2. *Octolasion
cyaneum* 3. *Eisenia rosea* and *Lumbricus rubellus*
4. *Apporectodea turgida* 5. *Eisenia fetida*

Ideas - Discuss why having a system for scientific
names is important. For example: It allows
scientists to communicate with each other.

Page 10
Answers - 1. *Dendrobaena octaedra*
2. *Allolobophora chlorotica* 3. *Eiseniella
tetraedra* 4. *Apporectodea longa*

Page 11
Answers - 1. *Acinonyx jubatus* 2. *Panthera pardus*
3. *Felis domestica* 4. *Panthera tigris* 5. *Lynx rufus*
6. *Panthera leo*

Page 12
Answers - 1. greenish 2. yellow 3. cyan
4. lavender 5. red 6. rosea

Ideas - For references, provide a standard
dictionary or an encyclopedia.

Page 13
Answers -

Bonus Activity : glow worm =firefly, an adult insect

Page 14
Answers - 1. 39 inches 2. .78 inches 3. 13.3 oz 4.
require a ladder to climb out 5. to help her
government decide whether it should be on the list
of endangered species 6. answers vary

Ideas - See metric conversion chart on page 168 to
assist in calculations.

Page 17
Answers - Part A. 1. 22 mm 2. 31 mm 3. 2.2 cm 4.
3.1 cm 5. 2.2 mm 6. 3.1 mm 7. 1.8 mm

Part B. salt, radish seed, cabbage seed, carrot seed
(answers may vary depending on seed size and
cocoon size)

Ideas - Collect samples of items listed in Part B so
that students may have hands-on experiences when
making size comparisons. Extend activity by
having students collect items that may be the same
size as a cocoon.

Page 18
Answers -

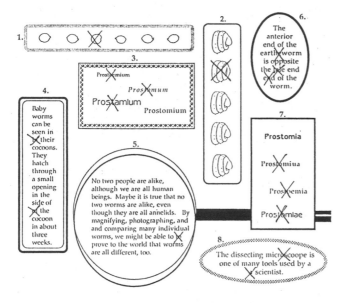

Ideas - Stress the concept that scientists need to develop good observation skills. This includes the ability to detect similarities (ways things are the same) and differences (ways things vary).

Page 21
Answers - 1. it gets thinner 2. it gets thicker 3. it gets shorter and fatter 4. it gets longer and thinner 5. they act as brakes

Page 23
Answers - 1. under a log, under a rock, on the sidewalk after a rain, in the garden, under moist leaves 2. it's damp; it's dark; food is present; oxygen is present; protected from predators 3. yes. conditions: water contains enough oxygen; there is food for the worms; there are no fish to eat the worms; there is no light 4. cold water can hold more oxygen than warm water

Ideas - Direct the students' attention to key ideas on activity page. The key ideas are the major concepts needed to answer questions.

Page 25
Answers - A.1. true 2. false 3. true 4. true; (Answers will vary in part B) B.1.a. they have 4 legs, 1.b. horses have hooves, 2.a. they have jointed legs, 2.b. millipedes have more than 8 legs, 3.a. both have red blood, mouths, digestive tracts, 3.b. cats are warm-blooded; worms are cold-blooded, 4.a. both have red blood, mouths, and digestive tracts; both require oxygen for their red blood, 4.b. birds have feathers, beaks, eyes, legs; worms do not.

Page 26
Answers - 1. deep in the ground or into the center of compost piles 2. they go deep in the ground beneath the frost line; the anti-freeze in their blood keeps them from freezing 3. they hibernate 4. under moist rocks or logs, down in damp earth 5. because they seek shelter 6. they seek shelter

Page 28
Answers -

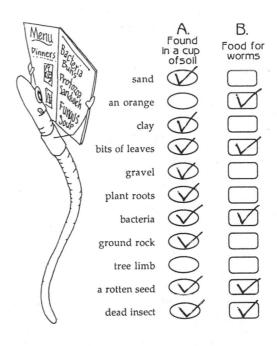

Page 29
Ideas - Air space, on the average, is equal to 25 percent of soil volume. Worm burrows help to increase the air volume.

Page 30

Answers - 1. 16 2. 4 3. 8 4. A 5a. oxygen; 6 molecules 6. carbon dioxide; 2 molecule

Page 31

Ideas - Can worms smell? They don't detect smells in the same way we do. However, they do have preferences in food and do sense a wide range of chemicals.

Page 33
Answers -

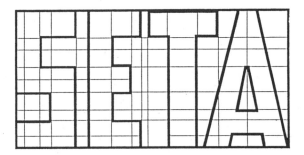

Page 34

Answers - 1. no; because the ground is frozen all the time 2. hot and dry 3. aboard ship in potted plants brought over by immigrants 4. yes; because lands along the equator contain many suitable environments (warm, moist, plenty of vegetation for food)

Ideas - Provide a globe and/or a world map for students to complete bonus activity.

Page 35
Answers - 1, 3, 5, 6, 4, 7, 2

Page 36
Answers -

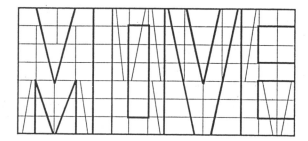

Page 38
Answers -

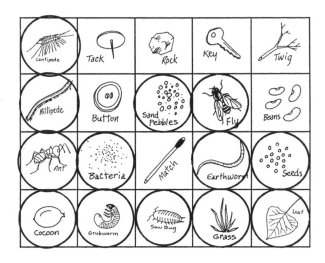

Page 39

Answers - 1. in the earth 2. summer and winter 3. cease to work 4. dry or frozen 5. at night 6. tail end 7. bristles 8. in their burrows

Page 41
Answers -

It's a Dirty Job

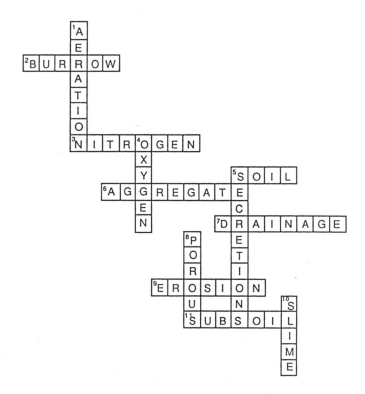

Page 42
Answers -

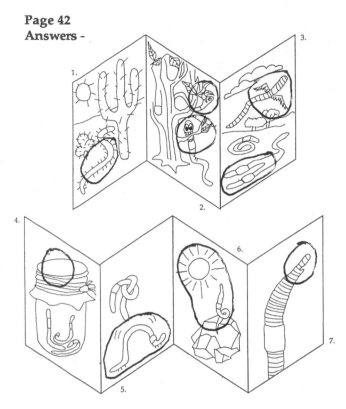

Ideas - Ask students to verbally state why they've circled each error. Some hints: 3. if severed, earthworms cannot grow two anteriors (heads), but can regenerate a few segments on both ends; 4. no air holes provided in top of jar; 5. worms can tie themselves in knots, especially to conserve moisture during hibernation; worms do not move like an inchworm which is an insect larva; 7. the worm's mouth is found in segment 1 of the anterior and not in segment 4 as shown.

Page 43
Answers - C = cold-blooded; W = warm-blooded

C turtle	C Texas horned lizard	W bird
W lion	C trout	W human
W horse	W kangaroo	W cat
C snake	W raccoon	C frog
C snail	C fish	C earthworm

Page 44
Answers -

ANIMALS		
W lemming	W starling	W shrike
W woodchuck	C sturgeon	W seal
C iguana	C gunnel	W gazelle
W pipit	W fisher	C alligator
W opossum	C skink	W skunk
W killer whale	W ermine	C cottonmouth
C gecko	W egret	C cobra

Bonus Activity: human average temperature = 98.6 deg. F, cat temperature = 101 to 102 deg. F, dogs = 100-101 deg. F, horse=99 deg. f, birds=106 deg. F

Ideas - Because the earthworm is cold-blooded, its temperature will be the same as its surroundings.

Page 45
Answers - 1. human 2. horse 3. worm 4. pigs 5. beak 6. skin 7. feathers 8. cold-blooded 9. a burrow 10. chick (Note: answers may vary as there are correct alternatives for some of the analogies, such as 5. beak or gizzard)

Page 46
Answers -

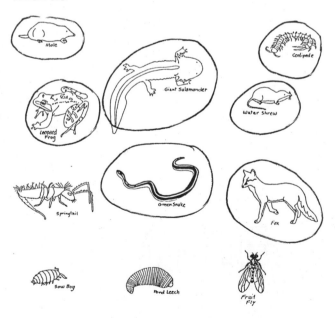

Ideas - Ask students to give reasons for their selections.

WORMS EAT OUR GARBAGE Copyright © 1993 Flower Press

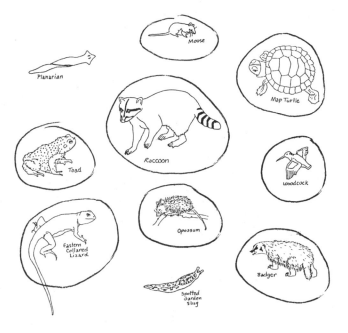

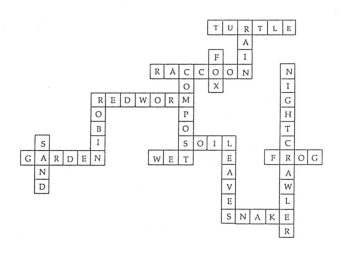

Ideas - Some interesting facts! Map turtles eat worms and other animals when they are young. As adults they are mainly herbivores (plant-eaters). The planarian, *Dugesia tigrina (6 mm or 1/4 inch)*, shown on the activity sheet does not eat earthworms. A predatory planarian, *Bipalium adventitium (70-150 mm or 3-6 inches)*, attacks earthworms and can be a serious problem in earthworm cultures. It is shown as a Soil Flatworm in the Food Web chart, page 89.

Page 48
Ideas - Instead of making this a cut and paste activity ask students to <u>write</u> names in the food chain links.

Page 49
Answers - 1. a sequence of who feeds upon whom 2. living things and their relationships to each other and their environment 3. DDT 4. answers will vary 5. we are part of the food chain; if we eat plants or animals with pesticides on (or in) them, we can become very ill

Ideas - Direct students' attention to the picture on the activity page. Present this interesting fact: if the parent fox does not model hunting of worms, the kits will not learn to do so.

Page 53
Answers - 1. warm 2. leaves. 3. moisture 4. setae 5. clitellum 6. anterior 7. blood
Bonus Activity - answer: BACTERIA

Pages 56- 58
Ideas - Use the story to introduce this section of the book, *Worms at Work*. The story can be presented in a variety of ways. Make copies for students to read individually or together in small groups. Read the story aloud to the class. Present a class play, *The Worm Who Came to Dinner*, with students acting out the parts.

Refer to pages 59 and 60 for activities that accompany the story.

Page 59
Answers - 1. newspaper 2. chart 3. rainy 4. clitellum 5. cocoon 6. moist; light 7. table scraps, garbage 8. basement 9. bait for fishing

Page 62
Answers -

1. Determine the size of the worm bin you will need.

2. Build the worm bin.

3. Put bedding in the worm bin.

4. Bury garbage in the bedding.

5. Add worms to worm bin.

6. Harvest castings to feed your plants.

7. Replace castings with fresh bedding.

Page 63
Answers - Items that do not belong in a worm bin: plastic bag, tin can, junk mail, glass jar, rubber band

Ideas - Some communities discourage including meat, dairy products, and bones in home worm bins, because they feel these items are more likely to produce odors and attract rodents.

An interesting fact: Earthworms are omnivores and, like humans, eat meat and plants.

Page 64
Answers - Responses may vary. These are examples: A-asparagus, B-banana, C-cracker, D-doughnut, E-eggshells, F-french fries, G-grapes, H-hamburger, I-ice cream, J-jelly, K-ketchup, L-lettuce, M-melon, N-nectarine, O-onion, P-peelings, Q-quince, R-radish, S-spaghetti, T-tamale, U-ugli fruit, V-vegetable, W-watermelon, X-xerographic paper (*If you can come up with a better one for X, please let us know!*), Y-yams, Z-zucchini

Page 66
Ideas - Glossy paper and paper with colored inks are not suitable for a worm bin because the color ink may be toxic to the worms. Also, paper coatings may be resistant to breaking down. Black ink is generally okay to use in a worm bin. Blue-lined notebook paper is okay because there is very little ink on the paper to be of harm to the worms

Page 67
Answers- 1. b 2. c 3. d 4. c **Bonus Activity**: no; they will need 15 lb of worms; 15,000 worms

Page 68
Answers -
1. 3:1 2. 3:1 3. 5:1 4. 5 worms 5. (drawings) 6. there are 4 Sow bugs to 1 Centipede or there is 1 Centipede to 4 Sow bugs. 7. 4:1 or 1:4 8. yes

Page 69
Answers - 1. 2 lb 2. .5 lb 3. 5 lb 4. 300 oz; 60 oz
5. 200 oz / 5 days = 40 oz garbage per day

Page 70
Answers - 1. 3.0 lb 2. 12 sq ft 3. 3.5 lb 4. 14.0 lb

Ideas - Have students calculate top surface area of the containers shown on the activity page.

After a bin has been set up for a least two months, it should be able to handle almost twice as much food waste each week as given in the chart. The worms grow in size and reproduce. More worms eat more garbage. After two months, you will need to add bedding to your bin. At four months you can harvest your worms by one of the several methods described in pages 90 and 91.

Page 74
Answers -

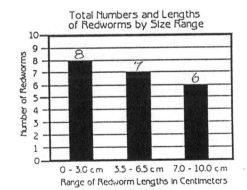

Total Numbers and Lengths of Redworms by Size Range

Tally Chart

Size Ranges	Tally Marks
0 - 3.0 cm	ЖЖ |||
3.5 - 6.5 cm	ЖЖ ||
7.0 - 10.0 cm	ЖЖ	

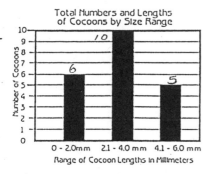

Total Numbers and Lengths of Cocoons by Size Range

Tally Chart

Size Ranges	Tally Marks
0 - 2.0 mm	卌 I
2.1 - 4.0 mm	卌 卌
4.1 - 6.0 mm	卌

Page 80
Ideas - Use the Worm Bin Record on page 162 to keep data on the worm bin over a period of time.

Page 81
Answers - 1. a. 45 b. 202 c. 12.6 d. 6.4 e. 4.5 f. 1.97 2. 68 to 81 deg. F; 78.3 deg. F 3. decomposing garbage produced heat 4. answers will vary

Ideas - Use the Project Planning Calendar on page 160 to calculate the number of days of the project. This calendar lists the number of days from the beginning of the year to any particular date. Its purpose is to help you determine experiment starting and ending dates and days when action needs to be taken.

Page 82
Answers - Part I. answers will vary Part II. prediction examples: if food is buried, it will disappear over a period of time; it will be necessary to add new bedding; if food waste is added to a worm bin, the temperature will increase

Ideas - Answers for Part I do not depend on having a worm bin. They depend upon having analyzed data in the Garbage Record on page 81. Part II requires a worm bin and its Worm Bin Record sheet on page 162 for completion. Encourage students to change their predictions into hypotheses, to develop experiments to test their hypotheses and to carry out their plans.

Page 83
Answers -

Increase Decrease

Increase	Decrease	
▲	☐	Feed the growing population more food.
☐	▼	Remove vermicompost containing worms.
☐	▼	Put a predator, such as a mouse or a frog, into the worm bin.
▲	☐	Add fresh bedding.
☐	▼	Put the worms in a smaller bin.
☐	▼	Place worm bin in hot sun.
☐	▼	Take away the food supply of the worms.
▲	☐	Build a bigger worm bin.
☐	▼	Let the worm bin dry out.
☐	▼	Remove some of the worms and go fishing.
☐	▼	Let the worm bin freeze.

Ideas-An intriguing chart giving mathematical projections for worm population increases is provided by Dr. Micheal Bisesi on page 190.

Page 84
Ideas - The activity has been designed to be completed in five days. Not all students will have worms hatch during that period of time. If necessary, make provisions for students to observe the cocoons longer.

Page 85
Ideas - Ask students to sequence the animals from largest to smallest. (Note: The animals are not drawn to scale.) One way to handle sequencing with the size ranges presented is to use the largest number in each range.

Page 86
Ideas - Students need to complete activity on page 85 before starting this one.

Pages 87 and 88
Ideas - These activity pages should be used together. Create your own activities based upon these pages. Include "who am I" questions that contain unique characteristics of the animals in a composting environment, and ask students to guess "who." Game Cards/Question Cards on page 169 are ideal for writing the questions and answers upon. Sample questions: Do I eat vegetation? Can I roll up into a ball?

Fruit flies can be a nuisance in a worm bin. Page 189 gives some suggestions on prevention, as well as how to catch them if they become a problem.

Page 89

Answers - 1. actinomycetes, molds, bacteria, beetles, white worms, earthworms, millipedes, sow bug, fly 2. roundworms, protozoa, springtails, mold mites, beetle mites 3. first-level consumer 4. second-level consumer 5. ground beetles, centipedes, ants, predatory mites, rove beetles

Ideas - Interesting fact: Green plants are called <u>producers</u> not <u>consumers</u> They store energy from the sun in the form of food. All consumers depend on plants for their sustenance. We humans are level one consumers when we eat plants, which are producers. When we eat meat, we are level three consumers.

Page 90

Ideas - Discuss the advantages and disadvantages of using this method for harvesting worms. The major advantages of this method are that it is easy and time-saving. A major disadvantage is that you will lose some of the worms. Most of them will die in the garden because redworms are not normally soil dwellers. While they are alive, however, they will work in the top of the soil and will eat vegetable litter and deposit castings. When the worms die they will add nitrogen to the soil because their decaying bodies contain nitrogen. This makes the soil fertile for plant growth.

Page 91

Ideas - Discuss the advantages and disadvantages of this method for harvesting worms. The advantages are that you can save a majority of the worms, keep good data (weigh and count worms), find cocoons to put back in the bin, harvest castings for garden flowers, and harvest worms for fishing or to start a new worm bin. The major disadvantage of this method is that it is time-consuming.

This is a great activity for a group of people. Tasks and observations can be shared.

Page 93

Answers - 1. false 2. true 3. false 4. true 5. false 6. false

Ideas - Ask students to rewrite false statements to make them true.

Page 94

Answers - 1. opinion 2. fact 3. opinion 4. fact 5. fact 6. fact 7. opinion 8. fact 9. opinion 10. opinion

Page 96

Ideas - Before introducing this activity, read the news article on page 95. Other activities related to the worm party are found on pages 97, 98, 99, and 100.

Page 100

Idea- Use a metal orange juice lids as a badge. Glue paper disk containing message inside the rim of lid. Tape a safety pin on the back. Thanks to Kim Davison for this idea.

Page 101

Ideas - Ask students to write a *bin-time* story, such as "Humans Make Good Worm Friends."

Page 102

Answers - 1. bedding 2. pill bug 3. earthworm (answers may vary) 4. organic waste 5. fruit flies 6. worm bin 7. white worm 8. cocoon

Ideas - Ask students to make their own riddles to share with classmates.

Page 104

Ideas - This is Melissa's story and should be used as an introduction to the activities on scientific experimentation, pages 105 - 111. Read it aloud to the class or provide copies for individual reading. Comprehension questions for the story are found on page 105. **Interesting fact**: Melissa Howe won first place with her worm project for outstanding achievement in 7th grade science from the Kalamazoo(MI) Association of Non-Public Schools, March 1992.

Page 105

Answers - 1. a. an educated guess about the outcome of an experiment b. a forecast about what will happen c. a person who studies natural phenomena in a systematic manner d. to agree to e. to refuse to accept 2. to test a hypothesis, a scientist collects data to determine if the hypothesis (educated guess) is true (accepted) or false (rejected) 3. wanted to find out which soils help multiply worms and which soils support worm growth 4. weighed the worms and measured the lengths of the worms 5. counted the worms and cocoons in the soil samples 6. no; results of the experiment were not included in this story

Page 106
Answers - 1. 13 worms 2. 1 worm 3. over 4 inches
4. 166.5 inches 5. 22 inches 6. 12.6 grams 7. 6.3
grams

Ideas - The data shown on this activity page (and
on pages 107 to 110) provide many opportunities for
analysis. Develop questions and activities to
assist students in comprehending the charts and
graphs.

Page 107
Answers - 1. .135 grams 2. no (one adult died)
3. yes (125 babies) 4. 174 (adults and babies)
5. 3 1/2 inches 6. 2 1/2 and over 4 inches long
Bonus Activity: yes; increased in length, weight,
and number

Page 108
Answers - 1. 41 worms 2. 4 worms 3. decreased; by
96.5 inches 4. similar distribution of short and long
worms but worm population decreased 5. 32 worms
6. no 7. no; there was a similar distribution of
short and long worms, but the total weight, length,
and number of the adult worm population had
significantly decreased

Page 109
Answers - 1. Clay 2. yes; Marl 3. Clay
4. A8 (Clay), B9 (Adrian Muck), C7 (Cass Sandy
Loam), D6 (Kalamazoo Sandy Loam), E1 (Fox
Sandy Loam), F2 (Spinx Sandy Loam), G3 (Clay
Loam), H4 (Houghton Muck), I10 (Control -
Newspaper), J5 (Marl)

Ideas - Discuss ways in which data can be
misleading. In this case, it appears that Clay soil
is the best soil for supporting worm growth. The
number of worms increased, but the total weight
decreased. Both conditions, increase in worm
population and increase in average worm weight,
must be met in order for a soil to be considered a
healthy environment for worms. Read Melissa's
results:

"Clay had the most population of all! What a
shock to find 400 worms!!! I could not believe we
found 337 babies. We did not find any babies for the
whole top three-fourths of the jar - the babies were
all at the bottom. The soil was like a rock and it
was hard to look through. The total weight
greatly decreased, with the average weight per
worm cut nearly in half." Also see Fact or Opinion
activity page 111 about worms in newspaper.

Page 110
Answers -

Change In Worm Populations Over a Four Week Period

A Soil type	B Beginning number of worms	C Ending number of worms	D Change in number of of worms	E Factor for population change	F Percent change
Fox sandy loam	50	175	+125	2.5	+250%
Houghton muck	50	140	+90	1.8	+180%
Marl	50	32	-18	-.36	-36%
Clay	50	395	+345	+6.9	+690%
Adrian muck	50	335	+285	+5.7	-570%

Adapted by permission from Melissa Howe

5. Which soil type showed the greatest change in population?___clay___

Page 111
Answers -

Fact	Opinion
✓	
	✓
	✓
	✓
	✓
✓	
✓	
✓	
	✓
✓	
	✓
✓	

Ideas - Students may have different views about
which statements are facts and which are opinions.
Allow students to present rationales for their
choices.

Some people may wonder why we use newspaper as
bedding in worm bins since it is obvious from
Melissa's soil study that newspaper did not support
the growth of worms. The purpose of a worm bin is
to get rid of garbage; the newspaper provides a
medium in which the worms can work. It does not
have to provide nutrients because the garbage does
that.

Page 113
Answers - 1. use no synthetic fertilizers and pesticides 2. - 7. answers are found in the Glossary 8. healthy soil in which billions of organisms live

Ideas - According to Dan Dindal who illustrated "Food Web of the Compost Pile," microbiologists have just changed the name for fungi-like bacteria from Actinomycetes to Actinobacteria.

Page 114
Ideas - Have students use page 116 on which to illustrate the soil profile.

Page 115
Answers - 1. O = 2 inches, A = 10 inches, B = 30 inches, C = 48 inches 2. 2 inches 3. 12 inches 4. 12 inches 5. 42 inches 6. 42 inches 7. 90 inches

Page 116
Ideas-The drawing on this page can be used with activity on page 119.

Page 117
Ideas-The Worm Observation Chamber can attract students' interest for several months, but water and food must be added regularly to provide a healthy environment for the worms and other soil organisms. This activity suggests adding at least two different kinds of worms. Nightcrawlers will tunnel deeply, redworms will be more likely to live in the organic horizon, and the garden worms will be more likely to make horizontal burrows in the topsoil. Review Tunnel Vision, page 119, prior to doing this activity. You may prefer to follow its procedure of adding one kind of worm at a time in order to be able to note its burrow locations before adding another kind of worm.

Another container for worm burrow observation: 1. Use a 2-liter plastic bottle. Cut off and discard the top. 2. Obtain a cardboard tube from a paper towel. Cut/punch holes in it to allow air in bottom of bottle. 3. Insert the cardboard tube vertically in the center of the bottle. 4. Fill with soil profile layers in the space around the outside of the tube. When the worms are placed in soil, they will be forced to live and tunnel near the outside of the bottle where it can be seen. Adapted from Kim Davison.

Page 118
Ideas - Have students use this log with the worm observation activity on page 117.

Note: Do **not** use corn meal to feed to the worms in worm observation activities. Although the worms would eat it, one scientist found that corn meal *on soil* can cause the growth of a fungus called *Aspergillus fumigatus*. This fungus can cause respiratory problems in humans.

Page 119
Ideas - Tunnel Vision utilizes the Worm Observation Chamber, page 117, to observe where different types of worms make their burrows and tunnels. Decide whether you want to add several kinds of worms at once, as on page 117, or whether you want to observe the behavior of one type of worm at a time, as in this activity. It may take several days to see evidence of worm burrows. Keep the fabric or cardboard cover over the chamber when observations are not being made so that worms will construct some burrows against the acrylic window. Worms will excrete castings inside their burrows, causing them to appear darker than the subsoil. A term for these casting-outlined burrows penetrating the soil is "worm-mottled soil." You will probably not be able to see discrete burrows in the organic horizon where the litter dwelling worms push organic layers aside. Reproduce the observation chart on page 161 and distribute it to students so they can document their observations. For a larger drawing surface for students, duplicate the worm observation chamber drawing without the directions on page 116.

Page 121
Answers - 1. c 2. g 3. a 4. f 5. d 6. e 7. b

Ideas - Discuss and clarify the job descriptions. Ask students to select a favorite worm and write their own work wanted descriptions. See pages 5, 8, 9, and 10 for worm types and descriptions.

Page 122
Answers - Worm Find Puzzle

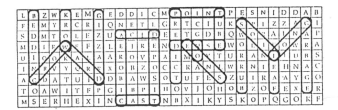

Page 123
Answers - 1. An earthworm can move a stone that is fifty times its own weight. 2. The giant earthworm of Australia may grow four feet long. 3. The Great Plains Indians called the full moon in the month of March the Full Worm Moon. 4. Composting toilets work better when redworms are present.

Ideas - The Great Plains Indians planted and harvested their crops according to moon cycles. One of these cycles was named the Full Worm Moon. During the Full Worm Moon earthworms begin to leave their castings behind and come to the surface, indicating that winter is over.

The Clivus Multrum composting toilet, invented in Sweden in 1937, is waterless and saves thousands of gallons of water without adding chemicals. The toilet uses natural biological decomposition to change raw human waste into odor-free compost that is like topsoil. Thanks to Abby Rockefeller for this information.

Page 126
Ideas - Obtain castings tea from a dry worm bin by placing the castings in a screened funnel over a jar and pouring water through them.

Other vegetables and flowers can be used for this experiment. Read seed packages for germination rates. See Resources/Enrichment, 191, for *Wisconsin Fast Seeds* ordering information.

Page 127
Ideas - City water may have enough chlorine in it to injure young plants. To make water safer for seedlings, let chlorinated tap water stand in an open container one or two days before using.

Don't overwater plants. Overwatering is a common cause of unhealthy plants. Overwatering causes the nutrients to wash away and fills up air spaces in the soil so the tiny roots don't get oxygen. If the soil surface is noticeably dry, then the plant needs to be watered.

Page 129
Idea- Do not use corn meal as food for worms in the Garbage Garden activities for reasons stated in Answer/Ideas #118 See comments for Page 130.

Page 130
Ideas - This activity is an extension of the Garbage Garden on page 129. Depending on the skill levels of your students, both activities can be introduced at the same time.

This experiment can become "smelly" if the bottle is overloaded with vegetable waste, or if there is a lack of air, or if it is too wet, or the experiment continues for more than one week. Some vegetables such as cabbage and broccoli smell worse than others as they decompose and should be avoided for use in the Garbage Garden. Use no meat waste.

Page 131
Answers -

Pages 132 and 133
Answers - 1. she counted 62 worms in one sq ft of soil; there are 43,560 sq ft in an acre; 62 x 43, 560 = 2.75 million worms per acre 2. 6.75 million worms in a hectare 3. .032 ounces or .915 grams 4. 65,340 oz or 4,084 lb 5. not only reduced soil, earthworm ,and microbial population but also the amounts of organic matter present in the soil 6. because worms are less active in dry and in cold weather they do not work 365 days of the year

WORMS EAT OUR GARBAGE Copyright © 1993 Flower Press

Page 134

Answers - 1. 16.0 2. 4.25 (rounded = 4.3) 3. 1.5
4. 7.25 (rounded = 7.3) 5. more food, moisture, and
oxygen were in some soils than in other soils

Ideas - Ask students to round off their answers to
the nearest tenth.

Page 135

Answers - (number of worms per square foot:
Kiesha = 25, Rosa = 50, Carrie = 60, Juan = 70,
Tony= 35, Jim = 30) 1. Juan 2. Kiesha 3. 40 worms
4. 50 worms 5. 45 worms **Bonus Activity:** 70 x 150 =
10,500 worms

Page 136
Answers -

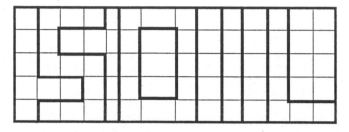

Page 138

Answers - Puzzle A: 1. cocoon 2. compost
3. vitamins 4. organic Puzzle B: 1. zero 2. light
3. feces 4. bait 5. aerobic **Bonus Activity:** Worm
castings fertilize plants.

Page 139
Answers -

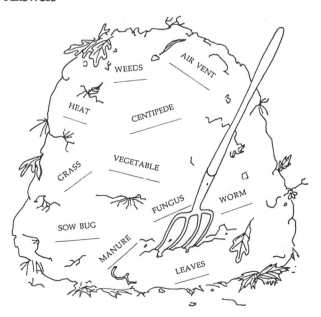

Page 142
Answers - **Recyler's Puzzles**

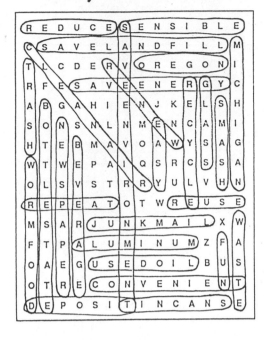

Page 143

Answers - A. metal wrench, milk jug, shoe, wheel
do not belong B. animals are not recyclable, a
broom can be plastic, however, the plastic may not
be recyclable, or the broom may be made of many
materials which cannot be easily separated for
recycling, a milk jug does not belong in the
newspaper box, dirt does not belong in a recycling
center

Page 147

Answers - 1. A person produces about two pounds of
garbage each day. 2. About forty percent of
curbside garbage is paper products. 3. Recycling one
ton of newspaper saves seventeen trees.

Ideas - Ask students to write interesting facts about
recycling in code. Share these messages with
classmates.

Page 148
Answers -

Page 152
Answers - 1. 154 lb of garbage eaten per day 2. 1,075 lb of garbage eaten per week 3. 56,210 lb of garbage eaten per year 4. save $2,248 per year.

answers calculated as follows:
359 households x 60% = 215.4 households with worm bins (round off number to 215);
215 households x 5 lb garbage per week = 1,075 lb garbage per week;
1,075 lb garbage per week ÷7 days per week =153.57 lb garbage per day (round off to 154);
154 lb garbage per day x 365 days per year = 56,210 lb per year;
56,210 lb per year ÷ 2000=28.105 tons;
28.105 tons x $80 per ton=$2,248.40
Answers may vary slightly depending upon where students choose to round off numbers.

Ideas-Such calculations are always estimates based upon samples with very wide ranges, so the actual number is less important than the range, often referred to as a "ball-park figure

Fruit Fly Trap

Worm bins occasionally develop a population of small flies--fruit flies, humpback flies, or black fungus gnats. Although in most cases these are more a nuisance than a problem, prevention is preferable to trying to get rid of them. Always cover garbage with bedding in the worm bin. Flies don't burrow into the bedding, so are less likely to lay eggs in the garbage if it is well-covered. Some people find that keeping food waste in a refrigerator prior to burial in a worm bin keeps the fly population under control. If a fly problem develops, a simple trap will attract large numbers of them. It doesn't totally get rid of them, but it does keep them somewhat under control.

Materials required: jar   plastic bag   fermenting fruit   rubber band

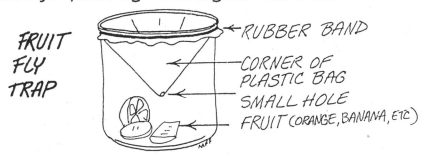

To make the trap, place the fermenting fruit in the jar with a small amount of water. Place the plastic bag over the mouth of the jar with one corner reaching down into the jar. Poke a small (no more than 1/4 inch diameter) hole in the corner of the jar with a pencil. Secure the bag around the rim with the rubber band. Flies will be attracted by the fermenting fruit, find their way through the tiny hole in the bottom of the funnel, and not be able to find their way out. You'll catch hundreds of them. Change the fruit/water solution every week by running hot water into the jar to kill any eggs and larvae which may develop.

Note: A chart for the mathematically inclined.

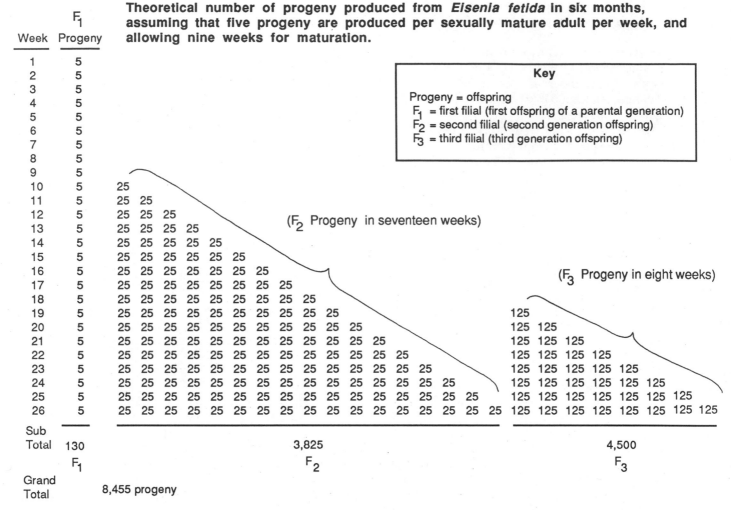

Theoretical number of progeny produced from *Eisenia fetida* in six months, assuming that five progeny are produced per sexually mature adult per week, and allowing nine weeks for maturation.

Key

Progeny = offspring
F_1 = first filial (first offspring of a parental generation)
F_2 = second filial (second generation offspring)
F_3 = third filial (third generation offspring)

(F_2 Progeny in seventeen weeks)

(F_3 Progeny in eight weeks)

Week	F_1 Progeny
1	5
2	5
3	5
4	5
5	5
6	5
7	5
8	5
9	5
10	5
11	5
12	5
13	5
14	5
15	5
16	5
17	5
18	5
19	5
20	5
21	5
22	5
23	5
24	5
25	5
26	5

Sub Total: F_1 = 130; F_2 = 3,825; F_3 = 4,500

Grand Total: 8,455 progeny

Data used with permission by Michael Bisesi

Notes:

1. Parent worm lays one cocoon per week from which 5 offspring hatch.

2. Over the 26 weeks, this yields 130 progeny (5 worms x 26 weeks = 130 worms). These are called the first filial, or F_1 generation.

3. At week 10, the first 5 offspring, now sexually mature, each produce 5 offspring (5 worms x 5 worms = 25). For the next 16 weeks, successive batches of offspring mature to produce their own progeny. All of these are called the second filial, or F_2 generation.

4. At week 19, the offspring from the first batch of worms in the F_2 generation mature, with each producing 5 offspring, for a total of 125 new offspring per week (25 worms x 5 worms = 125). These are called the third filial, or F_3 generation. For the remaining 7 weeks of the 26 week period, successive batches of F_3 offspring will mature, with each producing 5 offspring per week.

5. The total of all progeny, therefore is : F_1 (130) + F_2 (3,825) + F_3 (4,500) = 8,455 progeny.

Appendix C:
Resources and Enrichment Materials

For Teachers:

Appelhof, M. (1982). <u>Worms eat my garbage</u>. Kalamazoo, Michigan: Flower Press. The standard guide for how to set up and maintain a worm composting system. Highly recommended as a companion volume to <u>Worms Eat Our Garbage</u>. **For all ages**

Breckenridge, J. (1992). <u>Earthworms: Nature's recyclers</u>. Ottawa, Ontario: Harmony Foundation. An integrated unit about earthworms and worm farms; developed by a teacher. **Gr. K - 6**

California Association of Resource Conservation Districts. (1988). <u>Teacher's guide to the activity book: Amazing soil stories</u>. League City, Texas: National Association of Conservation Districts. An activity book designed to provide information on agricultural land and the environment. **Gr. 4**

Cohen, J., & Pranis, E. (1990). <u>GrowLab: Activities for growing minds</u>. Burlington, Vermont: National Gardening Association. An outstanding curriculum guide for use with an indoor classroom garden; contains a full range of hands-on activities designed to explore the world of plants. **Gr. K - 8**

Dindal, D. L. (1972) <u>Ecology of compost: A public involvement project</u>. Syracuse, New York: State University of New York College of Environmental Science and Forestry. A brief guide providing the basic principles of composting.

Dindal, D. L. (1980). <u>Decomposer food web</u>. Daniel Dindal, Box 54, DeWitt, New York 13214. A colorful and fascinating set of 70 slides with script describing the myriad creatures in a compost pile. **For all ages**

Ellis, T., & Scanlan, T. (1989). <u>Make a difference: Student activities for a better environment</u>. Toronto, Ontario: Is Five Press. A curriculum guide containing units on the topics: waste and energy management, transportation, and recycling.

Knott, R. C. Hosuome, K., and Bergman, L. (1989). <u>Earthworms teacher's guide</u>. Berkeley, California: University of California at Berkeley. Three 45 minute classroom activities observing earthworms and recording their pulse at different temperatures. **Gr. 6-10**

Kramer, D. C. (1989). <u>Animals in the classroom</u>. Menlo Park, California: Addison-Wesley Publishing Company. An excellent manual for selecting, preparing for, feeding, caring for, and handling animals including earthworms, reptiles, amphibians, fish, birds, mollusks, arthropods, snails and mammals. **For all ages**

McClure, G., & Stopha, P. (1991). <u>The great garbage concert: Environmental song and activity book</u>. Geneseo, New York: Glenn McClure. A delightful book that includes directions for recycling "trash" into musical instruments; clever songs to accompany Glen McClure's recording *The Great Garbage Concert for Kids*. **For all ages**

Metropolitan Toronto Works Department. (1990). <u>Here today, here tomorrow...revisited: A teacher's guide to solid waste management</u>. Toronto, Ontario: Author. An excellent curriculum with lesson guide and materials; designed to help students become aware of the problems involved in the management of solid waste; topics include recycling, composting, landfills, and incineration. **Gr. K - 8**

U. S. Soil Conservation Service. (1985). <u>Conserving soil: A practical teaching guide</u>. League City: Texas. Learning activities include digging in soils to see what (and who) is there, how native Americans used the land, and discovering current issues in soil conservation; photocopy activity masters for classroom use are available. **Gr. 6 - 9**

U. S. Soil Conservation Service. (1988). <u>Teaching soil and water conservation: A classroom field guide</u>. Washington, D. C.: Author. A content-packed guide to conservation and wise use of soil and moisture as a key to keep our land productive.

Source for Fast Sprouting and Growing Seeds

Wisconsin Fast Plants. Send for brochure to: Carolina Biological Supply Company, 2700 York Road, Burlington, North Carolina 27215

Source for Worm Bin and Worms

The Worm-a-way®. Flowerfield Enterprises, 10332 Shaver Road, Kalamazoo, MI 49002

For Students:

Ahlberg, J., & Ahlberg, A. (1990). <u>The little worm book</u>. New York: The Viking Press. A humorous view of worms with a real-life message; guaranteed to generate smiles and creative spin-offs.

Brennan, B. (Song Writer and Singer). (1984). <u>When my shoes are loose</u> (Cassette Recording). Takoma Park, Maryland: Do Dreams Music. A musical treat that will brighten your day; includes the song *Worms*.

California Association of Resource Conservation Districts. (1988). <u>Amazing soil stories</u>. League City, Texas: National Association of Conservation Districts. A comic book that carries the message: "Soil is too important to call dirt."

Coldrey, J. (1985). <u>Discovering worms</u>. Hove East Suffix BN3 1HF, England: Wayland Publishers. A beautiful and informative book that, with fantastic photographs, portrays the world of worms on land, in fresh water, and in the sea.

Dindal, D. (1993). <u>Food Web of the Compost Pile</u>. Daniel Dindal, Box 54, DeWitt, New York. 13214. A poster presenting an enlarged version of the <u>Food Web of the Compost Pile</u>.

Draper, A. S. (1988). <u>Adventures in the underworld: Book one - Herma builds a tunnel</u>. Dunnville, Ontario: Terra Publishing. The first story in a series about Herma, a young earthworm, and her thousands of families who live in the land that lies beneath us.

Diepenbrock, K. B. (1991). <u>Annelida: The wonder worm</u>. Oakland, California: Sagittarian Press. A delightful story about a worm; presents interesting content about earthworms and their contributions to the earth.

Handreck, K. A. (1978). <u>Earthworms for gardeners and fishermen</u>. Adelaide, Australia: CSIRO Division of Soils. A booklet about vermicomposting and earthworms: their habits, likes, and dislikes.

Handreck, K. A. (1978). <u>Organic matter and soils</u>. Adelaide, Australia: CSIRO Division of Soils. An informative summary of what is known about soil organic matter and what can be done to increase the amount of it in soil.

For Students (continued)

Hensley, T. J. (1978). <u>Animals without backbones: Investigations in science</u>. Toronto, Ontario: John Wiley and Sons. A student textbook with good background information about worms.

Jennings, T. (1990). <u>Junior science earthworms</u>. New York: Gloucester Press. A well-illustrated, easy-to-read book; includes interesting experiments to try; for the elementary level learner.

Kalman, B., & Schaub, J. (1992). <u>Squirmy wormy composters</u>. New York: Crabtree Publishing Company. All about red wigglers; colorful photographs and drawings illustrate worm bins in the elementary level classroom.

Lauber, P. (1976). <u>Earthworms: Underground farmers</u>. Champaign, Illinois: Garrard Publishing Company. A book with excellent photographs that relates the worm's life history to its ecological roles.

McLaughlin, M. (1986). <u>Earthworms, dirt, and rotten leaves</u>. New York: Macmillan Publishing Company. An award winning guide for gaining knowledge of earthworms and understanding the interconnections between living things and their environment; includes practical activities for exploration and experimentation.

Paulus, T. (1972). <u>Hope for flowers</u>. New York: Paulist Press. A classic story of life and its cycles; beautifully illustrated for children of all ages.

Penrose, G. (1982). <u>Dr. Zed's dazzling book of science activities</u>. Toronto, Ontario: Greey de Pencier Publications. A book of science experiments; includes activities involving a worm house, a bottle garden, and a solar sprouter.

Simon, S. (1969). <u>Discovering what earthworms do</u>. New York: McGraw-Hill Book Company. Covers topics from finding earthworms to earthworms in the soil.

Stwertka, E. (1991). <u>Rachel Carson</u>. New York: Franklin Watts. Describes the life and studies of Rachel Carson, highlighting her work and activities to save the environment.

Notes

_____

_____

_____

_____

_____

_____

_____

_____

_____

_____

_____

_____

_____

_____

_____

_____

_____

_____

_____

_____

_____

_____

_____

_____

_____

Bibliography

Appelhof, M. (1982). <u>Worms eat my garbage</u>. Kalamazoo, Michigan: Flower Press.

Barrett, T. J. (1959). <u>Harnessing the earthworm</u>. Boston, Massachusetts: Wedgwood Press.

Bisesi, M. (1993). <u>Theoretical number of progeny produced from *Eisenia fetida* in six months</u>. Unpublished chart. Medical College of Ohio, Occupational Health Program, Toledo, Ohio.

Buchsbaum, R. (1938). <u>Animals without backbones: An introduction to the invertebrates</u>. Chicago, Illinois: University of Chicago Press.

California Association of Resource Conservation Districts. (1988). <u>Teacher's guide to the activity book: Amazing soil stories</u>. League City, Texas: National Association of Conservation Districts.

Carson, R. (1962). <u>Silent spring</u>. Greenwich, Connecticut: Fawcett Publications.

Cohen, J., & Pranis, E. (1990). <u>GrowLab: Activities for growing minds</u>. Burlington, Vermont: National Gardening Association.

Darwin, C. (1898). <u>The formation of vegetable mould, through the action of worms, with observations on their habits</u>. New York: D. Appleton and Company.

Dindal, D. L. (1972). <u>Ecology of compost: A public involvement project</u>. New York: NY State Council of Environmental Advisors and the State University of New York College of Environmental Science and Forestry.

Edwards, C. A., & Lofty, J. R. (1977). <u>Biology of earthworms</u> (rev. ed.). London, United Kingdom: Chapman and Hall.

Edwards, C. A., & Neuhauser, E. F. (Eds.). (1988). <u>Earthworms in waste and environmental management</u>. The Hague, The Netherlands: SPB Academic Publishing.

Handreck, K. A. (1973). <u>Earthworms for gardeners and fishermen</u>. Adelaide, Australia: CSIRO Division of Soils.

Handreck, K. A. (1978). <u>Organic matter and soils</u>. Adelaide, Australia: CSIRO Division of Soils.

Hegner, R. W., & Stiles, K. A. (1951). <u>College zoology</u> (6th ed.). New York: The Macmillan Company.

Howe, M. (1992). <u>Worms: Growth in soils</u>. Unpublished manuscript.

Hunt, T. F., & Burkett, C. W. (1913). <u>Soil and crops with soils treated in reference to crop production</u>. New York: Orange Judd Company.

Lee, K. E. (1959). The earthworm fauna of New Zealand. (Bulletin 130). Wellington, New Zealand: New Zealand Department of Scientific and Industrial Research.

McLaughlin, M. (1986). <u>Earthworms, dirt, and rotten leaves</u>. New York: Macmillan Publishing Company.

Minnich, J. (1977). <u>The earthworm book: How to raise and use earthworms for your farm and garden</u>. Emmaus, Pennsylvania: Rodale Press.

Rathje, W., & Murphy, C. (1992). <u>Rubbish!</u> New York: Harper Collins Publishers.

Reynolds, J. W. (1977). <u>The earthworms (*Lumbricidae and Sparganophilidae*) of Ontario</u>. Toronto, Canada: Royal Ontario Museum.

Schaller, F. (1968). <u>Soil animals</u>. Ann Arbor, Michigan: University of Michigan Press.

Stwertka, E. (1991). <u>Rachel Carson</u>. New York: Franklin Watts.

U. S. Conservation Service. (1985). <u>Conserving soil: A practical teaching guide</u>. League City, Texas: National Association of Conservation Districts.

U. S. Conservation Service. (1988). <u>Teaching soil and water conservation: A classroom and field guide</u>. Washington, D. C.: Author.

Notes

_____

_____

_____

_____

_____

_____

_____

_____

_____

_____

_____

_____

_____

_____

_____

Glossary

acid A liquid that tastes sour and smells somewhat sharp. Acids help dissolve rock and break down food. Vinegar is an acid. It is a normal product of decomposition. Redworms do best in a slightly acid (pH less than 7) environment. Below pH 5 can be toxic. Addition of pulverized egg shells and/or lime helps to neutralize acids in a worm bin. See **pH**.

pH Scale <u>0   1   2   3   4   5   6   7   8   9   10   11   12   13   14</u>
                acid   neutral   alkaline

Actinomycetes Fungi-like bacteria. New name for this group is Actinobacteria.

aggregation Clustering, as when soil particles form granules that aid in aeration and or water penetration.

aeration Exposure of a medium to air which allows exchange of gases.

aerobic Pertaining to the presence of free oxygen. Organisms that utilize oxygen to carry out life functions.

air Mixture of atmospheric gases, including nitrogen, oxygen, carbon dioxide, and other gases in smaller quantities.

albumin A protein in cocoons that serves as a food source for embryonic worms. Also found in egg white.

alkaline Containing bases (hydroxides, carbonates) which neutralize acids to form salts. See **acid** and **pH**.

Allolobophora caliginosa One of the early scientific names for the species of earthworm now known as *Aporrectodea turgida*, the pasture worm.

Allolobophora chlorotica Scientific name for green worm. It may look green, but also may appear yellow, pink, or gray. Found in a wide variety of soil habitats, including gardens, fields, pastures, forest, clay, peat soils, lake shores and stream banks, and among organic debris. This species is generally a shallow burrower.

anaerobic Pertaining to the absence of free oxygen. Organisms that can grow without oxygen present.

animal A living being capable of sensing its environment and moving about. Animals live by eating the bodies of other organisms, whether plant or animal.

annelid Term for a member of the Phylum Annelida containing segmented worms.

anterior Toward the front.

Apporectodea trapezoides Scientific name for southern worm, commonly found in earth around potted plants, gardens, fields, forest soils, and banks of springs and streams. This worm lacks pigment. Its color is often lighter behind the clitellum, darkening to brown, brownish, or reddish brown towards the posterior. Flattening of body near posterior makes cross-section appear rectangular.

Apporectodea turgida Scientific name for pasture worm, commonly found in gardens, fields, turf, compost, and banks of springs and streams. This worm lacks pigment. The anterior may be flesh pink, the remaining segments pale gray.

aquatic Living in or upon water.

arctic Pertaining to the region around the North Pole.

bacteria Plural for bacterium, a one-celled organism which can be seen only with a microscope. Bacteria may be shaped like spheres, rods, or twisted springs. Some bacteria cause decay; others may cause disease. Most bacteria are beneficial because they help recycle nutrients.

bar graph Presentation of data using columnar blocks. Also known as a histogram.

barrier A geographic zone such as an ocean, desert, or glacier which would prevent the migration of an earthworm. Barriers may be different for other kinds of animals.

bedding Moisture-retaining medium which provides a suitable environment for worms. Worm beddings are usually cellulose-based, such as newspaper, corrugated cartons, leaf mold, or compost.

bio-degradable Capable of being broken down into simpler parts by living organisms.

biologist A scientist who studies living things.

biological control Management of pests within reasonable limits by encouraging natural predator/prey relationships and avoiding use of toxic chemicals.

blood A liquid medium circulating in the bodies of many animals. Blood carries food and oxygen to the tissues and carries waste products, including carbon dioxide, away from the tissues. Earthworms and humans both have a red, hemoglobin-based blood for oxygen transport.

breathe To carry on activities to permit gas exchange. Humans and land-dwelling vertebrates do this by expanding the lung cavity to draw air in, and reducing it to force air out. Worms conduct gas exchange through their moist skin, but do not actually breathe.

breeders Sexually mature worms as identified by a clitellum.

bristles Tiny rigid structures on most segments of earthworms which serve as brakes during movement. Known as setae, the patterns they form are a major distinguishing characteristic of earthworms.

burrow Tunnel formed when an earthworm eats its way through soil, or pushes soil aside to form a place to live and move more readily through the earth.

calcium carbonate Used to reduce acidity in worm bins and agricultural soils. See lime.

carbon dioxide Gas produced by living organisms as they utilize food to provide energy. Also produced through the burning of fossil fuels.

castings See worm castings.

castings tea A solution containing nutrients which dissolve in water in the presence of worm castings.

cellulose An inert compound containing carbon, hydrogen, and oxygen; a component of worm beddings. Cellulose is found in wood, cotton, hemp, and paper fibers.

centipede A predator sometimes found in worm bins. Centipedes have more than 8 jointed legs with one pair of legs attached to each of many segments.

classify To organize materials, organisms, or information based upon a defined set of characteristics.

clay As a soil separate, the mineral soil particles which are less than 0.002 mm in diameter. As a soil type, soil material that is 40% or more clay, less than 45% sand, and less than 40% silt. Clay has smooth particles and feels sticky when wet. Clay absorbs moisture readily.

climate The prevailing or average weather conditions of a place over a period of years.

clitellum A swollen region containing gland cells which secrete the cocoon material. Sometimes called a girdle or band, it is present on sexually mature worms.

---

cocoon Structure formed by the clitellum which protects embryonic worms until they hatch.

cold-blooded Having blood that varies in temperature approximating that of the surrounding air, land, or water. Fishes, reptiles, and worms are cold-blooded animals.

compost Biological reduction of organic waste to humus. Used to refer to both the process and the end product. One composts (verb) leaves, manure, and garden residues to obtain compost (noun) which enhances soil texture and fertility when used in gardens.

concentration In air or water, the strength or density of particles in a defined volume. The air we inhale has a higher concentration of oxygen molecules than carbon dioxide molecules.

consumer An organism that feeds on other plants or animals.

contract Action of muscle as it draws up, or gets shorter.

culture To grow organisms under defined conditions. Also, the product of such activity, as a bacterial culture. Vermiculture is growing worms in culture.

cyst A sac, usually spherical, surrounding an animal in a dormant state.

DDT A toxic pesticide found to accumulate in the food chain and cause the death of animals which were only indirectly exposed.

decompose To decay, to rot; to break down into smaller particles.

decomposer An organism that breaks down cells of dead plants and animals into simpler substances.

decomposition The process of breaking down complex materials into simpler substances. End products of much biological decomposition are carbon dioxide and water.

Dendrobaena octaedra Scientific name of earthworm known as the octagonal-tail worm. Found mostly in non-cultivated sites, such as in sod or under moss on stream banks, under logs and leafy debris, or in cool moist ravines. Also found in dung and in soil high in organic matter. A surface-dwelling species. Posterior is octagonal in cross-section.

dew worm The common name used by Canadians for *Lumbricus terrestris*, known to people around the world as the nightcrawler.

digestive tract The long tube where food is broken down into forms an animal can use. It begins at the mouth and ends at the anus.

dissect To cut open in order to examine and identify internal structures.

dissolve To go into solution.

dorsal The top surface of an earthworm.

earthworm A segmented worm of the annelid group which contains some 4000 species. Most earthworms are terrestrial that is, they live in the ground. Earthworms have bristles known as setae which enable them to burrow in the soil. Earthworms help to aerate and enrich the soil.

ecology The science of the interrelationships between living things and their surroundings.

egg A female sex cell capable of developing into an organism when fertilized by a sperm.

egg case See cocoon.

Eisenia fetida Scientific name for one of several redworm species used for vermicomposting. Color varies from purple, red, dark red to brownish red, often with alternating bands of yellow in between segments. Found in manure, compost heaps, and decaying vegetation where moisture levels are high. Frequently raised in culture on earthworm farms. See also *Lumbricus rubellus*.

Eisenia rosea Scientific name for worm known as the pink soil worm. Color is rosy or grayish when alive. During hibernation in cold winters and estivation during hot, dry summers, worm may be found in the soil tightly coiled in a small pink ball. Most common habitat is in soil under logs.

Eiseniella tetraedra Scientific name for worm known as the square-tail worm. Body is cylindrical anterior to the clitellum, square in cross-section behind the clitellum. The species shows a preference for damp habitats, having been found near wells, springs, underground waters, rivers, ponds, lakes, and canals. It has been found in bottom deposits of streams, lakes, and ponds.

enchytraeids Small, white segmented worms common in vermicomposting systems. As decomposers, they do not harm earthworms. Also called pot worms.

environment Surroundings, habitat.

excrete To separate and to discharge waste.

experiment To conduct research by manipulating variables to answer specific questions expressed as statements known as hypotheses.

feces Waste discharged from the intestine through the anus. Manure. Worm castings.

fertilize To supply nutrients to plants, or, to impregnate an egg.

food chain The sequence defined by who eats whom, starting with a producer (green plant).

food web The sequence defined by who eats whom, starting with producers and progressing through various levels of consumers, including decomposers and predators. Many organisms may be more than one level of consumer, depending upon whether they eat a plant, a microorganism which has consumed a plant, or an animal which ate the microorganism which ate the plant. A food web describes more complex linkages and interrelationships than a food chain.

Fungi A large group of plants having no green color and which reproduce by spores. The group includes mushrooms, toadstools, and microscopic plants including molds and mildew.

fungus A member of the plant group Fungi. The plural of fungus is fungi. Use fungi in reference to more than one plant, capitalize the term Fungi when referring to the major plant group.

garbage Wet discards, food waste, and offal, as contrasted with trash, which refers to discards that are dry.

genus A category of classification which groups organisms with similar characteristics. These are more general than species characteristics.

gland A specialized type of tissue which produces secretions. Glands in a worms' skin produce mucus.

girdle See clitellum.

gizzard Structure in anterior portion of digestive tract whose muscular contractions help grind food in the presence of grit.

hatchlings Worms as they emerge from a cocoon.

heart Muscular thickening in blood vessels whose valves control the direction of blood flow. Earthworms have several (commonly 5 pairs) of these blood vessels which connect the dorsal to the ventral blood vessels.

heavy metal Dense metal such as cadmium, lead, copper, and zinc which can be toxic in small concentrations. Build up of heavy metals in garden soil should be avoided.

hemoglobin Iron-containing compound in blood responsible for its oxygen-carrying capacity.

histogram A way of presenting data using columnar blocks. Also known as a bar graph.

humus Complex, highly stable material formed during breakdown of organic matter.

hydrated lime Calcium hydroxide. Do not use in worm bins. See lime.

hypothesis A prediction or educated guess which is used to guide a scientist in designing an experiment.

immigrate To move into a region.

inoculate To provide an initial set of organisms for a new culture.

larva Early form of any animal that changes structurally before becoming an adult. A caterpillar is an insect larva which becomes a moth or butterfly as an adult.

leach To run water through a medium, causing soluble materials to dissolve and drain off.

leaf mold Leaves in an advanced stage of decomposition.

lime A calcium compound which helps reduce acidity in worm bins. Use calcium carbonate, ground limestone, egg shells, or oyster shells. Avoid caustic, slaked, and hydrated lime.

limestone Rock containing calcium carbonate.

litter (leaf) Organic material on forest floor containing leaves, twigs, decaying plants, and associated organisms.

loam A rich soil composed of clay, sand, and some organic matter. Soil material that is 7% to 27% clay particles, 28% to 50% silt particles, and less than 52% sand particles. The organic matter acts like a sponge to hold water.

Lumbricidae Name of family group to which several redworm and nightcrawler species of earthworms belong.

Lumbricus rubellus Scientific name for a redworm species. Color is ruddy-brown or red-violet, iridescent dorsally, and pale yellow ventrally. It has been found in a wide variety of habitats, including under debris, in stream banks, under logs, in woody peat, in places rich in humus, and under dung in pastures. Grown in culture by worm growers.

Lumbricus terrestris Scientific name for large burrow-dwelling nightcrawler. Also known as the nightcrawler, Canadian nightcrawler, or dew worm.

macroorganism Organism large enough to see by naked eye.

marl A crumbly soil consisting mainly of clay, sand, and calcium carbonate.

mate To join as a pair; to couple.

Mecascolides australis Scientific name of the Giant Gippsland Earthworm of Australia, one of the largest earthworm species in the world.

membrane A tissue barrier capable of keeping some substances out and letting others in.

microorganism Organism requiring magnification for observation.

microscope, dissecting An instrument permitting magnification of organisms too small to see clearly with the naked eye, but too large for a light microscope.

mineral A naturally occurring substance found on the earth which is neither animal nor plant. Minerals have distinct properties such as color, hardness, or texture.

mineral soil Soil that is mainly mineral material and low in organic material. Its bulk density is greater than organic soil.

mold A downy or furry growth on the surface of organic matter, caused by fungi, especially in the presence of dampness or decay.

molecule The smallest particle of an element or compound that can exist by itself. Two atoms of oxygen make up a molecule of oxygen. Two atoms of oxygen and one atom of carbon make up a molecule of carbon dioxide.

muck Dark colored, finely divided, well-decomposed organic soil material mixed with mineral soil. The content of organic matter is more than 20%. Muck has the least amount of plant fiber to bulk density, and the lowest water content of all organic soil material when saturated with water.

mucus A watery secretion, often thick and slippery, produced by gland cells. One function is to keep membranes moist.

muscle Tissue made of specialized cells whose main function is to contract.

nematodes Small (usually microscopic) roundworms with both free-living and parasitic forms. Not all nematodes are pests.

nightcrawler A common name for the worm *Lumbricus terrestris*. Often called the Canadian nightcrawler in the United States, or dew worm in Canada.

nitrogen An odorless, colorless, tasteless gas which makes up nearly four fifths of the earth's atmosphere. When it combines with oxygen through the action of nitrogen-fixing bacteria, it can become incorporated into living tissue as a major part of protein.

nocturnal Coming out at night.

nourish To promote or sustain growth.

Octolasion cyaneum Scientific name for the woodland blue worm. Body is octagonal in the posterior. It is blue-gray or whitish, and found in damp locations, including under stones in water, in moss, and on stream banks.

Oligochaeta Name of the class of annelids to which earthworms belong, characterized by having setae.

optimal Most favorable conditions, such as for growth or for reproduction.

organic Pertaining to or derived from living organisms.

organic matter Material which comes from something which was once alive.

organism Any individual living thing.

ovary Organ which produces eggs.

overload To deposit more garbage in a worm bin than can be processed aerobically.

oxygen Gaseous element in the earth's atmosphere essential to life as we know it.

patio bench worm bin Worm bin, usually wooden, large and study enough to use as a bench on the patio.

peat moss Sphagnum moss which is mined from bogs, dried, ground, and used as an organic mulch.

pest An organism which someone wants to get rid of.

pesticide A chemical, synthetic or natural, which kills pests.

pH An expression for degree of acidity and alkalinity based upon the hydrogen ion concentration. The pH scale ranges from 0 to 14, pH of 7 being neutral, less than 7 acid, greater than 7, alkaline.

pH Scale 0 1 2 3 4 5 6 7 8 9 10 11 12 13 14
                    acid   neutral   alkaline

pit-run Worms of all sizes, as contrasted with selected breeders.

plant An organism which is green at some stage of its life and which uses the energy from sunlight to produce its own food. Plants do not move about on their own. An oak tree is a plant.

pollute To make foul or unclean, to contaminate.

population The total number of individuals of a single species in a defined area.

population density Number of specific organisms per unit area, e.g. 1000 worms per square foot.

posterior Toward the rear, back, or tail.

potting soil A medium for potting plants.

pot worms See enchytraeids.

prostomium Fleshy lobe protruding above the mouth of an earthworm.

protein Complex molecule containing carbon, hydrogen, oxygen, and nitrogen; a major constituent of meat. Worms are approximately 60% protein.

protozoa Plural for protozoan, a one-celled organism belonging to the animal kingdom. Most protozoa live in water and can be seen only with a microscope. Some move by means of tiny hairs called cilia, others by a whip-like tail called a flagellum, and others by false feet called pseudopodia like amebas have.

ratio A fixed relationship, expressed numerically, as in a worm:garbage ratio of 2:1.

redworms A common name for *Eisenia fetida* and also *Lumbricus rubellus*. *Eisenia fetida* is a common worm used for vermicomposting, although in some parts of North America, *Lumbricus rubellus* is more common.

regenerate To replace lost parts.

respire To exchange oxygen and carbon dioxide to maintain bodily processes.

salt Salts are formed in worm bins as acids and bases combine, having been released from the decomposition of complex compounds.

sand Loose, gritty particles of disintegrated rock ranging in size from 0.05 mm to 2.0 mm in diameter. Soil that is 85% or more sand and not more than 10% clay is classified as sandy soil. Sandy soil particles feel gritty. Water drains quickly through sandy soil.

scientist A person who studies natural phenomena in a systematic manner.

secrete To release a substance that fulfills some function within the organism.

segments Numerous disc-shaped portions of an earthworm's body bounded anteriorly and posteriorly by membranes. People identify earthworm species by counting the number of segments anterior to the position of structures such as the clitellum, ovaries, or testes. Segmentation is a characteristic of all annelids.

setae Bristles on each segment used in locomotion.

sexually mature Possessing a clitellum and capable of reproducing.

silt As a soil separate, individual mineral particles that range in diameter from the upper limit of clay (0.002 mm) to the lower limit of very fine sand (0.05 mm). As a soil textural class, silt is 80% or more silt and less than 12% clay.

slime Mucus secretion of earthworms which helps to keep skin moist so that gas exchange can take place.

soil Soil is made up of mineral particles, organic matter, air, and water. The mineral particles are called sand, clay, or silt, depending on their size. Sand has large particles and feels gritty. Clay has fine particles and feels sticky or slippery when wet. Silt particles range between clay and very fine sand. Soil types have differing amounts of each of these particles. Loam is a mixture of sandy soil, clay, and organic matter. The organic matter acts like a sponge to hold water.

southern worm Common name for *Aporrectodea trapezoides*.

sow bug A small crustacean with 10 pairs of legs which breathes with gills and lives in organic litter.

species Basic category of biological classification, characterized by individuals which can breed together.

sperm Male sex cells.

sperm-storage sacs Pouches which hold sperm received during mating.

springtail A small primitive insect with a turned-under projection on its abdomen which causes it to spring about.

stress To produce conditions which cause an organism to experience discomfort.

subsoil Mineral bearing soil located beneath humus-containing topsoil.

taxonomist A scientist who specializes in classifying and naming organisms.

terrestrial Living on land.

testis (plural, testes) Organ which produces male sex cells (sperm).

top dressing Nutrient-containing materials placed on the soil surface around the base of plants.

toxic Poisonous, life-threatening.

trash Refers specifically to discards which are theoretically dry, such as newspapers, boxes, cans, and so forth. The term is commonly used to indicate anything we throw away, including organics. With increasing emphasis on recycling, less material should be thrown away as trash.

turgid Swollen, distended, pressing out against sides.

ventral Term for the underneath surface of an earthworm.

vermicompost Mixture of partially decomposed organic waste, bedding, worm castings, cocoons, worms, and associated organisms. As a verb, to carry out composting with worms.

vermiculture The raising of earthworms under controlled conditions.

vibration A rapid, rhythmic motion back and forth. Earthworms are sensitive to vibration.

warm-blooded Having warm blood and a constant natural body heat which is specific for each species. Mammals and birds are warm-blooded.

white worms See enchytraeids.

woodland blue worm Common name for *Octolasion cyaneum*.

worm bedding The medium, usually cellulose-based, in which worms are raised in culture, such as shredded corrugated cartons, newspaper, or leaf mold.

Worm-a-way® worm bin Plastic worm bin which provides a method for aeration in lower parts of the bin. Patented invention designed by Mary Appelhof.

worm bin Container designed to accommodate a vermicomposting system.

worm casting Undigested material, soil, and bacteria deposited through the anus. Worm manure.

worm:garbage ratio Relationship between weight of worms and garbage used in a bin to convert the garbage to a useful end-product.

Index

Notes

Flowerfield Enterprises
10332 Shaver Rd. Kalamazoo, MI 49002
616-327-0108 FAX 616-343-4505

Products List

Item	Price	Shipping	U.S. $ Encl.
Worm-a-way ®			
Mary Appelhof's patented vermicomposting bin with ventilation system. Made from recycled plastic. Comes with book, **Worms Eat My Garbage,** plastic garden fork, and 1 lb of redworms. (Worm shipments depend on weather. Allow 3-4 weeks.)			
•**Model 7003**	$77.00	$8.00	_____
Capacity: 3 to 5 lb garbage/week Size: 20" x 24" x 12"			
•**Model 7002**	67.00	6.00	_____
Capacity: 2 to 3 lb garbage/week Size: 19" x 16" x 12"			
Redworms			
1 pound	17.00	4.00	_____
2 pounds	30.00	6.00	_____
Worms Eat My Garbage			
• **Book** by Mary Appelhof	8.95	1.50	_____
• **T-Shirt**	11.00	2.00	_____
100% cotton Adult sizes (Circle) S M L XL XXL			
• **Button**	1.00	.50	_____
Leaf Composting Video	25.00	3.00	_____
Backyard gardeners make compost pile of oak leaves with manure as nitrogen source, then place finished compost on garden in fall. 28 min.			
Children's Activity Book	19.95	2.00	_____
Worms Eat Our Garbage: **Classroom Activities for a Better Environment.** 4-8+ grades; 232 pp			

Michigan residents add 4% sales tax on items (less shipping).   _____

Make checks payable to **Flowerfield Enterprises**.   Total: _____

Ship to: (Include street address for UPS shipments.)

Name _____ Phone (_____)_____

Organization _____

Address _____

City/State/Zip_____

UPS zones 2,3,4. Surcharge for zones 5 or further. Prices good through January 1994

WORM·A·WAY ®

Patented

The **Worm-a-way** ® is Mary Appelhof's invention. This simple, yet effective system turns food waste into potting soil with the help of redworms. Many people consider her book, **Worms Eat My Garbage**, to be the definitive guide to vermicomposting. She makes worm composting even more convenient with her recycled plastic bin, the **Worm-a-way** ®, containing its unique aeration system. All you do is place moistened bedding, some soil, and a starting colony of redworms in the bin. You then bury kitchen waste in the bedding where bacteria and other organisms break it down. The worms eat the food waste, bedding, and bacteria, turning everything into nutrient-rich humus for use in your garden and house plants.

Each Worm-a-way ® kit includes:

✓ One ruggedly designed, plastic **Worm-a-way** ® vermicomposter with snap-on lid. Manufactured from recycled materials.

✓ One 100-page book, **Worms Eat My Garbage** by Mary Appelhof, a biologist and well-known expert in worm composting.

✓ Two easy-to-install ventilation tubes, four tube end vents, and two lid vents.

✓ Plastic garden fork.

✓ **Worm-a-way** ® assembly instructions and set up guide.

Why have worms eat your garbage?

✓ Turn garbage into fertilizer and ecycle organics back to the earth

✓ Grow worms for fishing

✓ Avoid contaminating recyclables

✓ Save energy with worm energy

✓ Reduce odor in garbage in cans

✓ Reduce need for landfills

✓ Use worms for science projects

Ordering Information			
Model	Size	Capacity	Price
7002	19" x 16" x 12"	2-3 lb garbage per week	$73.00
7003	20" x 24" x 12"	3-5 lb garbage per week	$85.00

Price includes 1 lb worms and shipping.   Michigan residents add 4% sales tax.

Make checks payable to:
Flowerfield Enterprises •10332 Shaver Road • Kalamazoo • Michigan 49002 • USA
Phone: 616-327-0108 FAX 616-343-4505

Mary Frances Fenton

Mary Appelhof

Author of *Worms Eat My Garbage*, 1982, Mary is recognized as an international authority and lecturer on small-scale vermicomposting. As owner of Flowerfield Enterprises and Flower Press, she has dedicated the past 20 years to research, development, and marketing of products related to the earthworm such as the Worm-a-way® worm bin for which she holds both Canadian and USA patents. Mary has won many honors. She received a National Science Foundation grant, was an invited speaker at the Global Assembly of Women and the Environment, and received special merit recognition as one of Renew America's Environmental Success Stories. Mary also coordinated the international research conference, Workshop on the Role of Earthworms in the Stablization of Organic Residues and compiled its preceedings. An award-winning photographer, she holds master's degrees in education and biological sciences and taught high school biology.

About the Authors

Mary Frances Fenton

Illustrator of *Worms Eat My Garbage*, 1982, Mary Frances, now retired, was an associate professor in the College of Education, Western Michigan University, where she directed an audiovisual media graphics service for 29 years. She holds a BFA in Design, University of Oklahoma, and a MA in the Teaching of Art, WMU, and has successfully competed in juried exhibitions in a three state area with watercolor paintings, bronze sculpture, and photography. Mary Frances has directed historical research projects on women in education and women artists. She brings many of her interests and talents to bear in this book. An avid gardener, she is a certified organic grower in Michigan.

Mary Appelhof

Mary Frances Fenton

Barbara Loss Harris, Ph. D.

Dr. Barbara Harris has co-authored numerous activity books for teachers including *Special Kids's Stuff, I've Got Me and I'm Glad*, and *People Need Each Other*, Incentive Publications. Barbara is an associate professor in the College of Education, Western Michigan University where she trains teachers of gifted and talented students and those with special needs. She holds degrees from the University of Florida and a doctorate from Wayne State University. She was a post-doctoral fellow at Michigan State University in 1992-93 where she studied school reform at Holt High School, an exemplary Professional Development School, Holt, Michigan. In addition to her daughter, Jennifer, and two exotic birds, Barb's interests include vermicomposting in the classroom, curriculum development, and research in the area of assessment and diagnosis of exceptional individuals.

 Flower Press is commited to publishing books designed to help people regain control over their own lives. By developing skills, sharing knowledge, and working cooperatively, we can accomplish together what none of us could do alone.